Malcolm MacGregor

The Divine Authority of Paul's Writings

Malcolm MacGregor

The Divine Authority of Paul's Writings

ISBN/EAN: 9783337779313

Printed in Europe, USA, Canada, Australia, Japan

Cover: Foto ©Lupo / pixelio.de

More available books at **www.hansebooks.com**

The Divine Authority
of Paul's Writings.

BY

MALCOLM MACGREGOR, D.D.

WITH AN INTRODUCTION BY

HENRY McDONALD, D.D.

"*If any man thinketh himself to be a prophet, or spiritual, let him take knowledge of the things which I write unto you, that they are the commandment of the Lord.*"   *PAUL.*

Atlanta:
THE FOOTE & DAVIES COMPANY,
PRINTERS AND BINDERS.
1898.

TO THE MEMORY

OF

JOHN A. BROADUS, D.D., LL.D.

SOMETIME PRESIDENT OF THE SOUTHERN BAPTIST THEOLOGICAL SEMINARY,

WHOSE LOFTY CHRISTIAN CHARACTER, RARE ATTAINMENTS IN CHRISTIAN LEARNING, AND GREAT ACHIEVEMENTS IN CHRISTIAN WORK HAVE SHED A LUSTRE OVER CHRISTIAN SCHOLARSHIP, AND PROVED A STIMULUS TO CHRISTIAN TOIL, AMONG THE BRETHREN OF HIS OWN AND OTHER DENOMINATIONS,

THIS BOOK IS DEDICATED

IN GRATEFUL REMEMBRANCE OF HIS INTEREST IN, AND APPROVAL OF, ITS PLAN AND SUBSTANCE, AND HIS ENCOURAGEMENT TO THE AUTHOR TO COMPLETE AND PUBLISH IT.

PREFACE.

This work is an attempt to supply, in condensed form, what appears to be a real and recognized want—a study of the claims of Paul to absolute apostolic authority, and the scope of that authority over modern thought and life. Though various learned treatises have dealt, in a fragmentary way for the most part, with different aspects of the subject, there appears to be no one work which presents the subject comprehensively and concisely. The writer has aimed at suggestiveness, rather than exhaustiveness, of treatment. In the prosecution of the work, he has been encouraged, by not a few brethren distinguished for their attainments and their loyalty to the truth, to hope that in several respects, and in some measure, this little volume may prove helpful to the cause of New Testament Christianity. For this he is truly thankful. It only remains to be said that nearly all the Scripture quotations in the book are made from the Revised Version; and that the few other Scripture quotations are made from the Authorized Version.

MALCOLM MACGREGOR.

ATLANTA, April, 1898.

CONTENTS.

INTRODUCTION.

CHAPTER.   PAGE.

I.—NEED OF THE DISCUSSION.—Sure foundation necessary to safe superstructure. Christianity founded on Old Testament and New Testament Scriptures. Large part of New Testament written by Paul. Inspiration and apostolic authority of Paul vitally important. Ancient and modern anti-Paulinism. 17

PART ONE.

BASAL POSITIONS.

II.—NATURE OF THE APOSTOLIC OFFICE.—Christ's appointment and training of "the twelve" for office. Apostles had infallible guidance of the Spirit. Their words were his words. They were official witnesses of Christ's resurrection. Chief organs of divine revelation in new dispensation. Determiners of Christian faith, ethics, and polity. Their precepts the statute law, and their example the common law, of the churches. Divinely attested by gift of inspiration and power of miracle-working. 27

CHAPTER.	PAGE.

III.—GENUINENESS OF PAUL'S APOSTLESHIP.—All "signs of an apostle" present in Paul. Had "seen the Lord." Was appointed and instructed exclusively by Christ himself. Wrought many mighty miracles and had full inspiration. Was "caught up into Paradise." Defends his apostleship in Galatian and Second Corinthian letters. Mutual testimony of Peter and Paul. Harmony of Paul and James.   51

IV.—EXTRAORDINARY CHARACTER OF PAUL'S APOSTOLIC MISSION.—His mission to plant pure Christianity in Gentile lands. His great qualifications for the work. Special relations and adaptations of his apostleship to Gentile peoples.   72

V.—APOSTOLICITY OF PAUL'S WRITINGS.—Writing necessary to permanence of apostolic teaching. Divine authority and impulse to write. Significant groups of Pauline Epistles. Letters of Paul apostolic in design and force. Paul commands churches, prophets, and pastors. Alleged admissions of occasional non-inspiration of Paul answered.   82

PART TWO.
PRACTICAL BEARINGS.

VI.—PRACTICAL BEARING ON CHRISTIAN HISTORY. Epistolary correspondence the best source of history. Letters of Paul, and "Acts," by his companion, the principal data of early Christian history.   III

CHAPTER.	PAGE.

VII.—PRACTICAL BEARING ON CHRISTIAN DOCTRINE. Characteristic Pauline doctrines. Fulness of Paul's teaching. System of Christian doctrine established by Paul's writings. 114

VIII.—PRACTICAL BEARING ON CHRISTIAN ETHICS. Relations of history, doctrine, and ethics. Pauline ethics, wide in range and lofty in character. Writings of Paul enlarge and confirm Christian ethics. 118

IX.—PRACTICAL BEARING ON CHURCH ORDER.—Indebted almost exclusively to Paul and his companion, Luke, for light on church order. 121

SECTION I. NATURE OF THE CHURCH.—Church universal and invisible composed of aggregate of finally saved. Church local a self-governing body of believers. Departures from New Testament order. . . . 124

SECTION II. OFFICERS OF THE CHURCH.—Apostles and evangelists in relation to the work at large. Bishops (pastors) and deacons the only officers of the local church. Functions of pastors and of deacons. Importance of training for the "business" of the diaconate. Ignoring the model. . . 132

SECTION III. POSITION OF WOMAN IN THE CHURCH.—Pauline prohibitions of women's speaking in the church. Great positiveness and agreement of exegetes on subject. Womanly modesty and good taste acquiescing. Answers to objections. 143

| CHAPTER. | PAGE. |

X.—PRACTICAL BEARING ON ESTIMATE OF CHRISTIAN ATTAINMENTS.—Professions of high attainments and superior light to be tested by Paul's writings. Origen. *Illuminati.* Quakerism. Swedenborgianism. Mormonism. Spiritualism. "Christian Science." Christian Consciousness, etc. . 173

APPENDIX.

I.—THE FIVE-LINKED CHAIN.—A Study of a Group of Pauline Doctrines in Romans 8: 29, 30. 207

II.—DIVINE ESTIMATE OF PASTORAL OFFICE. . . 227

INTRODUCTION.

Dr. MacGregor has wisely discerned the salient position around which another battle must be waged for the truth as it is in Christ. In Paul's own day there were those that resisted his message by the denial of his apostolicity. It was a direct, positive and ultimate assault. If Paul was not an apostle, there was an end of the authority which gave a divine sanction to his teaching. This early opposition furnished the opportunity for the fullest assertion and clearest vindication of his claim to the extraordinary office to which he was called by the personal appointment of the Lord Jesus.

"Old foes with new faces" verifies

itself in that the modern assailants of the nineteenth century are as determined to minimize the influence of Paul as were his antagonists of the first century. Hence the present volume," The Divine Authority of Paul's Writings."

The Pauline Epistles, with their contents, are constantly assailed by all sorts of opposers — some formidable by their display of learning, others almost contemptible by their show of ignorance. At no time has a thorough discussion of the whole subject been more necessary than in the present. The old plea of Romanism, maintaining a succession of men in the apostolic office, has long ago overthrown the authority and teachings of the real apostles, and substituted for the word of God the traditions of men. Many who deem themselves far away from the great error of Rome are drifting into the same destructive tendency. Every enthusiast who has a theory or organization to spring upon the world, for which no support, or against which no positive prohibition, is found in the Bible, finds it easy to make the charge that the writings of the New Testament were simply provisional and temporary. In the times of this ignorance, God winked at this well-meaning antique delusion, but the nineteenth century — this latter day of Messiah — has come, and Who are the apostles? especially, Who is Paul? that we should bow our necks to the bondage of the environments of that early time.

The author's selection of his theme and manner of discussion is wise and timely. With reverence and courage, with vigor and clearness, he restates the fundamental truths in regard to the apostolic office — the appointment of Paul, his authority in his extraordinary commission, and the apostolicity of his Epistles. These positions are vital. They are supported not by fiery denunciations, but by calm argument and fair, lucid statement. You feel that the foundation is true and abiding. Paul is still the great apostle of the Gentiles, "even as our beloved brother Paul also according to the wisdom given unto him hath written unto you . . . . in which are some things hard to be understood, which they that are unlearned and unstable wrest, as they do also the other Scriptures, unto their own destruction."

The second part consists in the statement and discussion of the practical bearings of the basal positions which have been so strongly sustained in the first five chapters.

We have only to look at these practical bearings to see how far-reaching and instructive they are. On church history, on Christian doctrine, on Christian ethics, on church order (nature of the church, officers of the church, position of woman in the church), and on estimate of Christian attainments.

Possibly the discussion of woman's position in the church may interest more people by reason of the present agitation of this subject. All the chapters, however, are instructive and profitable. While the book is specially adapted to the present and should be read by thoughtful people in all of our churches, I am glad to say that to all churches it commends itself by its breadth of view and the nature of the subject, free from anything denominationally offensive.

It would prove an admirable book for a course of study in our young people's various societies.

Dr. MacGregor has done his work well. He shows that the pulpit is not the only sphere in which he can do splendid work. His scholarly culture, his profound reverence for the truth of God, his lucid terseness of style, have enabled him to write a book by which he may hope to help the faith of the children of God in holding the great verities of revealed truth. May its circulation be worthy of its merits.

HENRY MCDONALD.

ATLANTA, April, 1898.

The Divine Authority of Paul's Writings.

Chapter I.

NEED OF THE DISCUSSION.

Without a sure foundation, no structure, whether material, mental, moral, or religious, can be safe. The superstructure is imperilled quite as much by assaults upon the foundation as by direct assaults upon itself. To undermine the foundation is to demolish the superstructure.

Genuine Christianity, with its glorious economy of salvation, with its sublime facts, doctrines, and ethics; with its significant ordinances, simple but effective church organization and polity, and vast scheme of work and worship, is based exclusively upon the Old and New Testaments; and, for obvious reasons, very specially upon the New Testament. It is "built upon the foundation of the apostles and prophets, Christ Jesus himself being the chief corner stone." Without the Scripture there can be no Christianity. Unless the authority of Scripture be firmly established, Christianity can have neither definiteness, power, nor stability.

The divine inspiration and consequent infallibility of the Sacred Writings are, therefore, of vital importance to the Christian religion. The absolute inerrancy of the Holy Scriptures is fundamental to their own authority and claims, and to our certainty of mind in matters of Christian truth and duty. The unimpeachable and perfect truth of the Sacred Writings, as established by their clearly proved divine inspiration, together with their explicit, implied, and oft-repeated claims, must be held to, immovably, as a first principle of genuine Christianity, and as a *sine qua non* of progress and assurance in the knowledge of divine things. To this prime and impregnable position, all our theories of the nature of divine inspiration, and of the relations between the divine and human elements in the products of inspiration, must conform; or we must discard theory upon the subject, while boldly accepting the revealed facts.

The inspired word is explicit enough with regard to its own origin, character, and claims. "The sweet psalmist of Israel" said, "The spirit of the Lord spake by me, and his word was upon my tongue."[a] The prophet Jeremiah averred, "The Lord said unto me, Behold, I have put my words in thy mouth."[b] Inspired wisdom has declared, "Every word of God is

[a] 2 Sam. 23: 2.   [b] Jer. 1:9.

pure."[a] In one form or another, the Apostle Paul has asserted substantially that "All Scripture is given by inspiration of God."[b] The Apostle Peter has told us concerning inspiration, that "Men spake from God, being moved by the Holy Ghost."[c] The Saviour himself has said, that the "word is truth," and that "the Scripture cannot be broken."[d] On the divine origin, absolute inerrancy, and supreme authority of the Holy Scriptures, these and kindred testimonies are indisputable and final.

A very large and exceedingly important portion of the New Testament was written by the Apostle Paul. More than one-fourth of the bulk, and about one-half of the books, of the New Testament, were written by him. It is significant also that more than one-half of the sacred writing known

[a] Prov. 30: 5.   [b] 2 Tim. 3: 16.   [c] 2 Peter 1: 21.
[d] John 10: 35.

to us as "The Acts" of the Apostles is simply a record of the sayings, doings, and experiences of Paul, as the Lord's great apostle to the Gentiles.

While no portion of either the New Testament or of the Old has been exempt from the assaults of infidel and semi-infidel critics, it is both strange and ominous that there should appear in various quarters, in current times, a disposition on the part of many who are not confessedly sceptical, but who claim to be essentially, or even eminently, Christian, to speak slightingly and even sneeringly of the Apostle Paul and his Epistles, and to act in disregard, or in defiance of him and of them. Most of these anomalous Christians fail to realize the disloyalty and lawlessness of their conduct; and were they once clearly to discern the true nature and actual tendency of their course, they would recoil from it as convulsively as they would from downright infidelity. This class of dissentients not only admit, but maintain, in general terms the divine inspiration and authority of all the Sacred Writings, and their difficulty with Paul is simply their inherited or acquired dislike for certain of his teachings and injunctions, the force of which they are struggling with great inconsistency to evade, or the meaning of which, on account of preconceived notions, they endeavor to modify, or explain away. But their course in this matter is perilous to their own Christian faith and loyalty, and, through the contagiousness of their example, perilous to the Christian faith and loyalty of others.

But there is another class of anti-Pauline dissentients, fewer, indeed, in number, but more adroit and malignant in their hostility, some of them in influential positions, who see clearly enough that their rejection of either much or little of Paul's teachings and injunctions can be justified only by partial or complete disestablishment of the divine inspiration and apostolic authority of the great apostle; and these fundamental claims, they do not hesitate, covertly or openly, to disparage and impugn. Prepossessions of rationalistic philosophy, the blinding influence of unscriptural customs, and the warping force of adventurous love of novelty, overweening self-conceit, and headstrong self-will account very fully for most of this dangerous anti-Pauline drift.

In the apostle's own day, chiefly in the church of Corinth and in the churches of Galatia, there were those who had the gracelessness and the temerity to question and belittle Paul's apostolic authority in the face of overwhelming proofs; but manifestly from the record they were the most unspiritual, pretentious, ambitious, designing, contentious, unscrupulous, and troublesome among all who at that time professed the Christian faith; and their course was vehemently repudiated by the better quality and great majority in the Christian communities.

These presumptuous and arrogant despisers of Paul's divinely constituted authority and mission made great boasts of their prophetic and spiritual gifts and attainments. For the sake of the gospel truths and institutions intrusted to him, Paul overcame the natural modesty of his disposition, and, in his Corinthian and Galatian letters, powerfully asserted and defended his independent, divinely bestowed apostleship; and we should be profoundly thankful for the vast amount of invaluable information concerning Paul's apostleship thus providentially furnished to the world. In the counsels of God, these men doubted that we might be assured. The saying of Paul which constitutes the pith and the motto of this little work is a crucial test of, and a crushing retort to, these would-be great ones—these self-seeking and presumptuous impugners of high apostolic authority: "If any man thinketh himself to be a prophet, or spiritual, let him take knowledge of the things which I write unto you, that they are the commandment of the Lord."[a] This test would prove the genuineness or the spuriousness of their much-boasted prophetic and spiritual gifts.

The things which the apostle wrote, referred to in this passage, are not merely those things contained in the immediate context; but they include all the rich and varied themes so fruitfully treated throughout this great Epistle and all the contents of all his Epistles.

[a] 1 Cor. 14:37.

In view of the ancient, and especially of the modern, anti-Pauline hostility, it will be well to examine the grounds on which we hold the divine authority of Paul's writings. For "if the foundations be destroyed, what shall the righteous do?" If one of the main supports of our Christian faith be weakened or removed, on what can it be based instead? We shall find, however, that the divine authority of Paul's writings rests ultimately and securely on four massive, closely related, and impregnable basal truths—the nature of the apostolic office, the genuineness of Paul's apostleship, the extraordinary character of Paul's apostolic mission, and the apostolicity of Paul's writings.

PART ONE.
BASAL POSITIONS.

Chapter II.

THE NATURE OF THE APOSTOLIC OFFICE.

The term "apostle" primarily signifies "one sent;" but even in the Old Testament, the term "sent" came to mean, in certain well-defined cases — as in the commissioning of Moses and Isaiah, "the sent of God" — the sent of God on a special mission, with special powers, to speak and write and act for God, with fullness of divine authority. The term "apostle" is used several times in the New Testament in a non-technical sense, as in the case of Barnabas. In a pre-eminent way, Christ himself is called in the Epistle to the

Hebrews, "the Apostle .... of our profession."

Early in his public ministry—in its first year, in fact—Christ chose the term to designate the holder of an extraordinary and all-important office, which he was about to institute among his disciples.

In some sort of parallelism with the "twelve princes" and "seventy elders" divinely appointed for the guidance and government of ancient Israel, Christ chose his "twelve apostles," and, about a year afterwards, "seventy others," of subordinate and unnamed office, to aid him in accomplishing his work among the Jewish people. Of all the evangelists, Luke alone, and only in one brief passage in his Gospel,[a] tells us anything of "the seventy;" and they are never again referred to in the New Testament.

The work of "the seventy" was con-

[a] Luke 10: 1-20.

fined, for the most part, if not altogether, to the last year of our Lord's personal ministry on earth before his crucifixion; and it was apparently designed to facilitate the completion of Christ's prophetic work, his work as preacher and teacher, before his rapidly approaching departure through his atoning death. When the Lord appointed "the seventy," he "sent them two and two before his face into every city and place, whither he himself was about to come."[a]

Of the Saviour's appointment of his twelve apostles, and of their work previous to his death, the account of Mark is as follows: "And he appointed twelve, that they might be with him, and that he might send them forth to preach, and to have authority to cast out devils."[b] But the most characteristic, and by far the most important, part of the work of the apostles was

[a] Luke 10: 1.   [b] Mark 3: 14, 15.

to be done after Christ's resurrection and ascension. The preparation of these twelve chosen men, by a special course of instruction and training, under himself personally, to be followed by extraordinary gifts and infallible guidance of the Holy Spirit, for the higher duties of their office, may be said to have been the chief, the central work of Christ's earthly ministry, considered apart from his work of atonement. Christ's preparation of "the twelve" was the training of teachers, leaders, and rulers. His training of them was not primarily a training for ideal saintship and seraphic personal holiness; but a training for office, for the peculiar and special work of apostleship, by which Christianity was to be fully formed, formulated, extended, and made permanent.

Christ selected these twelve men from among his followers, and set them apart, that they might be with him constantly, as heart-sympathizers with him in his temptations and trials, as ear-witnesses of his public discourses and private instructions, and as eye-witnesses of his majesty, of his mighty works, and, above all, of the crowning and most convincing miracle of his career—his resurrection from the dead—in order that, by these and other means, they might be specially prepared to act as his witnesses, spokesmen, and vicegerents, after his departure from the world.

After the ascension of Christ and the descent of the Spirit, the apostles were invested with several new and transcendently important functions.

In the first place, they were divinely required, through all their subsequent lives, to act as official and responsible witnesses of Christ's resurrection. "Ye are witnesses of those things,"[a] said Christ to them. "We are his

[a] Luke 24: 48.

witnesses of these things,"[a] said the apostles to their hearers. It is written, also, that, " with great power gave the apostles witness of the resurrection of the Lord Jesus."[b]

Christianity was fact before it was doctrine; and it is doctrine before it becomes life. Considered as history, as doctrine, as ethics, and as salvation, Christianity rests mainly on the resurrection of Christ. All is secure if that is proved; if that is disproved all fails. Hence the divine appointment of the apostles as special witnesses of this basal fact; and hence the overwhelming proofs they constantly furnished of that supreme event, and the great stress they laid upon it. Christ's resurrection, besides certifying a future life, proved Christ's divinity;[c] and his entire system of doctrine and ethics, whether personally or apostolically uttered; attested the genuineness, completeness,

[a] Acts 5: 32.   [b] Acts 4: 33.   [c] Cf. Rom. 1: 4

and efficacy of his atoning sacrifice; proclaimed his power to save; and warranted and invited the confidence of mankind in him as the Divine Redeemer.

Again, the apostles were constituted the chief, the supreme, organs of divine revelation in the new dispensation. As Christ's declaration that "the Scripture cannot be broken" assures us of the divine inspiration and infallible truth of the Scriptures of the Old Testament; so his promise of the transcendent aid and direction of the Holy Spirit to the apostles, to the effect that their utterances would be, not their words, but the words of God, assures us of the divine inspiration and infallible truth of the Scriptures of the New Testament.

Assuming the virtual, if not the actual, Pauline authorship of Hebrews, then with the scarcely more than seeming exceptions of Mark and Luke, who were apostolically endorsed companions and helpers of Peter and Paul respectively, and with the merely minor exceptions of James and Jude, the Apostles, Matthew, Peter, John, and Paul, were the writers of the New Testament. Through the revelation of Christ and the inspiration of the Spirit, the apostles determined the doctrines, the ethics, and the institutions of Christianity. In common with many other persons in the apostolic churches, who, as we are informed in the Acts and the Epistles, possessed prophetic gifts, Mark, Luke, James, and Jude must have exercised the prophetic function, at least in the form of inspiration, whether in the form of revelation or not. But the apostolic office, while it included the prophetic function in all its forms, was superior to, and authoritative over, that of the New Testament prophets, and, therefore, over the ordinary office of pastors and teachers and every other office whatsoever. All this is plainly indicated by Paul's statement, "God hath set some in the church, first apostles, secondly prophets,"[a] and by Paul's exercise of authority over prophets, in restricting their utterances to the requirements of order: "Let the prophets speak by two or three, and let the others discern. But if a revelation be made to another sitting by, let the first keep silence;"[b] and it is indicated more positively still by Paul's making the divine authority of his writings a test of the genuineness of claims to the gift of prophecy and other spiritual gifts: "If any man thinketh himself to be a prophet, or spiritual, let him take knowledge of the things which I write unto you, that they are the commandment of the Lord."[c]

The apostles, acting for Christ and by his authority, were the supreme de-

[a] 1 Cor. 12: 28.   [b] 1 Cor. 14: 29, 30.   [c] 1 Cor. 14: 37.

terminers of what should be taught and believed and done in the churches of Christ. They were the qualified and responsible agents and supervisors for Christ, in every department of church activity. The expressed or implied sanction or *imprimatur* of any of them would at once determine the canonicity of any writing. Each of them equally, and not Peter alone, had the keys of the kingdom of heaven; and whatever any of them bound or loosed on earth was accordingly bound or loosed in heaven. They were the authorized representatives, ambassadors, spokesmen, scribes, vicegerents, legislators, and judges for Christ in his church on earth; so that whatever they said, or did — not, indeed, in their personal and private capacity, but in their official capacity — was the veritable word and deed of Christ speaking and acting through them.

Special promises of extraordinary supernatural aid, in the discharge of their apostolic functions, were repeatedly made to them by Christ. On four separate and special occasions — first, when at the outset of their ministry, Christ commissioned the apostles to preach the kingdom of God; again, when Christ himself preached his gospel to a vast concourse of people; yet again, when he pronounced judgment upon Jerusalem and the Jewish nation; and once more, in his valedictory discourse — the Saviour made these wonderful promises of divine aid. "But when they deliver you up, be not anxious how or what ye shall speak: for it shall be given you in that hour what ye shall speak. For it is not ye that speak, but the Spirit of your Father that speaketh in you." [a] "The gospel must first be preached unto all the nations. And when they

[a] Matt. 10: 19, 20.

lead you to judgment and deliver you up, be not anxious beforehand what ye shall speak: but whatsoever shall be given you in that hour, that speak ye: for it is not ye that speak, but the Holy Ghost." [a] "Settle it therefore in your hearts, not to meditate beforehand how to answer: for I will give you a mouth and wisdom, which all your adversaries shall not be able to withstand or to gainsay." [b] "I have yet many things to say unto you, but ye cannot bear them now. Howbeit when he, the Spirit of truth, is come, he shall guide you into all the truth: for he shall not speak from himself; but what things soever he shall hear, these shall he speak: and he shall declare unto you the things that are to come. He shall glorify me: for he shall take of mine, and shall declare it unto you." [c]

It would be inconceivable that the

[a] Mark 13: 10, 11.   [b] Luke 21: 14, 15.   [c] John 16: 12-14.

divine aid thus promised on these occasions to the apostles should be vouchsafed when they spoke, and not, as some have ventured to allege, when they wrote; that it should be granted them when they spoke to a few persons, and withheld from them when they wrote concerning the great facts, doctrines, duties, privileges, and hopes of the gospel and kingdom of Christ, for all mankind, and for all time. But as a matter of fact, the apostles claim absolute and divine authority for their official words whether written or spoken. Thus Peter speaks of the apostolic letters, as well as of the apostolic oral utterances, as "the commandment of the Lord and Saviour through your apostles;"[a] and thus Paul declares, "the things that I write unto you . . . . . are the commandment of the Lord."[b] Thus also Paul exhorts the Thessalonians, "So then,

[a] 2 Pet. 3: 2.   [b] 1 Cor. 14: 37.

brethren, stand fast, and hold the traditions which ye were taught, whether by word, or by epistle of ours." [a] Absolute subordination to Christ who revealed his truth and will to them, and absolute authority over Christ's people for whose instruction and government Christ qualified and appointed them, were the fundamental characteristics of apostleship.

Further, the apostles were the authorized agents of Christ in founding, organizing, working, and governing the churches according to his will, as he supernaturally revealed it to them, and supernaturally aided them in carrying it out. On the very day on which the promised Spirit of God descended upon, and took full possession of, the apostles, completing their supernatural qualifications and sealing their divine authority, they began the organization of the first Christian

[a] 2 Thess. 2: 15.

church. The pattern which they thus set and the principles which they thus exhibited were to be the rule for the founding, working, and governing of all churches till the end of time. As the Book of Acts clearly implies, what the apostles said and did, in their official capacity, and, therefore, under the power of the Holy Ghost, was really what Christ continued "to do and to teach" after his ascension to the right hand of power.

All secular laws may be classified as common law, or statutory law; the former constituted by immemorial custom and the decisions of the courts, the latter by the acts of legislative bodies. Similarly, the divinely inspired examples and the divinely inspired precepts of the apostles, who alone were the lawmakers of Christianity, constitute respectively, the common law and the statute law of Christian life, and of the churches of

Christ; and each form of the revealed will of Christ is as binding as the other. Apostolic patterns and apostolic commands are of equal and of absolute authority. Thus the inspired example of the apostles, in holding the meetings of the churches for Christian worship and service, and for commemoration of the resurrection of Christ, on the first day of the week, rather than on the seventh, is as strong authority for the observance of "the Lord's Day" as the sacred day, as could be furnished by an inspired precept.

In the work of inspiration, the Divine Spirit had full and absolute mastery of all the faculties of the apostles and other inspired penmen; yet he worked in and through each of them in accordance with their particular natures and without destroying or ignoring their individuality. As a master musician will preserve the individuality of the various instruments on which he plays, while displaying fully his own individuality and genius in his use of each of them, and in combining them all harmoniously, as in an orchestra; so the inspiring Spirit, while preserving the individuality of each Scripture writer — the violoncello strains of Matthew, the stirring tabor beat of Mark, the peaceful flute notes of Luke, the trumpet peal of Peter, the clarion ring of James, the bugle tones of Jude, the violin and harp music of John, and the full organ diapason of Paul—exhibits his own dominant divine individuality, in each of them, and in producing the full harmony of the entire orchestra of inspiration.

Should it be asked, as it sometimes is, "How could God secure infallible presentation of his truth, while breathing it through the souls of fallible men?" it may be answered that he who brings being out of nothingness, light out of darkness, life out of death, order out of confusion, good out of evil, and who formed the sinless human nature of Christ out of the sinful nature of the virgin, could as readily secure the perfect presentation of his truth through minds that he prepared, sublimed, took possession of, and infallibly moved, directed, and controlled for that very purpose. Left to themselves, in their private personal capacities, these men must needs be fallible enough; but when grasped, permeated, inspired, moved, and managed by the infallible Spirit of God, they must needs be as infallible as himself.

It was necessary to the apostolic office, that the recipient of it should have "seen the Lord;" that he should be able to bear personal witness to the resurrection of Christ; that he should have received his apostolic commission from Christ himself, personally;

and that he should be able to exhibit the "signs of an apostle," in the exercise of supernatural gifts and powers, attesting his apostolic appointment, message, and mission. Thus, from the very nature of the case, the apostolic office, like the Melchizedek order of priesthood, was unique, and without succession. It could neither be evolved out of, nor be merged into, another office. In view of this, how presumptuous, absurd, and vain are the pretensions of those who claim to be officially the successors of the apostles, as if there could be any other real and true apostolic succession than that of keeping the apostolic doctrines, ordinances, and precepts as "once for all" they were delivered! The apostles had, and could have, officially, neither predecessors, nor successors; neither equals, nor substitutes. The duration of the apostolic office was, in fact, somewhat less than a full ordinary lifetime — from Christ's appointment of the apostolate, A. D. 31, till the death of John under Trajan, A. D. 100, a period of sixty-nine years.

The apostolic office was furnished with adequate divine sanctions and endowments for the due attestation of its genuineness, and for the full exercise of vitally important functions. In accordance with the promise of Christ, as we have already seen, the apostles had complete divine revelation and inspiration — the former, a supernatural communication of knowledge to them; the latter, a supernatural communication of either natural or supernatural knowledge through them to others—whereby they became, in their official capacity, through Christ and his Spirit, infallible organs of divine thought and will. They were, also, divinely invested with miraculous powers of the most remarkable character, to prove the truth, the divine origin, and divine approval of their message and their mission. "Many wonders and signs were done by the apostles;"[a] "God also bearing witness with them, both by signs and wonders, and by manifold powers, and by gifts of the Holy Ghost, according to his own will."[b] In attestation of their apostleship and of the truth of their message, they had the power to work miracles of great variety, marvelousness, and significance; and when occasion required, they had the power to enable other persons, on whom they laid their hands, to work miracles also; though the ability to impart miraculous powers to others they reserved exclusively for themselves. It was only through the laying on of the apostles' hands that the Holy Ghost was given. Thus it would appear, from the nature of the case, that the miracles of the Christian dispensation

[a] Acts 2: 43.   [b] Heb. 2: 4.

must have been confined to the apostolic age — at most to the lifetime of those Christian survivors of the apostles, on whom the apostles had laid their supernaturally gifted hands — which accords with the divine procedure under the old dispensation, in limiting miracles, for the most part, to the confirmation of newly delivered prophecies, or other authoritative expressions of the divine mind and will. Great as he was, in character and in mission, John the Baptist, the forerunner of Christ, wrought no miracle;[a] perhaps, in order that the wide distinction between Christ and himself might be more readily perceived, and, most probably, also because the chief work of John the Baptist was, not to announce essentially new truth, but to collect, condense, and focalize the Messianic promises and predictions, in "the law and the prophets" which

[a] John 10: 41;

had already been supernaturally attested; to announce their speedy fulfillment and the near approach of the Messiah; and to summon the people to prepare therefor, by genuine repentance. But Christ and his apostles, having important new truth to declare and an entirely new order of things to establish, freely employed miracles of great variety and power, to attest the truth of their claims and the divineness of their mission. It is to be observed in this connection, that, in one particular, miracles are like creative acts. Both are for the beginnings of things — the latter in the kingdom of nature, the former in the kingdom of grace.

The apostles were divinely furnished with supernatural wisdom, to enable them infallibly to detect hypocrisy, treachery, lying, simony, and similar evils, lurking in the bosoms of spurious professors of the new faith; and they were invested with divine authority to pronounce and execute summary judgment upon desperate transgressors, as in the case of Peter[a] declaring and carrying out the judgment of the Lord upon Ananias and Sapphira, and as in a similar instance in the ministry of Paul.[b]

In view of the nature of the apostolic office, as essentially a duly certified organ of divine utterance and action, the spoken or written words of an apostle must be regarded as of absolutely divine authority.

[a] Acts 5: 1-11.   [b] Acts 13: 9-11.

Chapter III.

THE GENUINENESS OF PAUL'S APOSTLESHIP.

All the qualifications and "signs of an apostle" were abundantly present in Paul. It is true, he had not been the companion and pupil of Christ during his earthly ministry, as were the other—"the twelve"—apostles. Their special mission to the Jewish people, particularly those of Palestine, among whom, exclusively, Christ had lived and ministered, made it necessary that they should have been thus privileged. So when it became needful for them to ascertain the divine choice and appointment of a disciple to take the apostleship rendered vacant by the sin and doom of Judas, Peter, the readiest of the eleven, said, "Of the men, therefore, which have companied with us all the time that the Lord Jesus went in and went out among us, beginning from the baptism of John, unto the day that he was received up from us, of these must one become a witness with us of his resurrection."[a] After prayer and the casting of lots, "Matthias was numbered with the eleven apostles," "to take the place in this ministry and apostleship from which Judas fell away."[b]

The Pentecostal outpouring of the Spirit not having as yet occurred, it was necessary for them to resort to this device divinely sanctioned by the Levitical law in particular cases, to obtain a clear expression of divine appointment of a new apostle, and on the other hand, it was necessary that the new apostle among the twelve should be divinely appointed before the Pentecostal descent of the Spirit that he might share in common with

[a] Acts 1: 21, 22. [b] Acts 1: 25, 26.

the rest of the twelve, in the extraordinary gifts and blessings of that momentous day. The coming of the enlightening, inspiring Spirit made it unnecessary for them ever again to resort to that or any similar expedient; and his coming revealed no error in their single use of it, but confirmed it, and certified the divine action in the premises in response to their call.

But while it was necessary, for the reason already indicated, that each of the twelve apostles should have been a constant companion of our Lord, virtually from his baptism to his ascension, it was not necessary that Paul, whose mission was to be to peoples among whom Christ had never lived, should have been thus circumstanced. Yet, even in Paul's case, though he was not of the twelve, but held an independent apostleship, personal acquaintance with Christ was necessary. [a]

[a] 1 Cor. 15: 8.   1 Cor. 9: 1.   Acts 22: 14, 15.

So we find that he had a full equivalent for acquaintance with Christ in his earthly life. He had "seen the Lord," not merely after his resurrection, but after his ascension. The risen and ascended Christ made a special revelation of himself to Paul. While all the other apostles, and more than five hundred private Christians, saw Christ after his resurrection and before his ascension, only Stephen, the first martyr, and John, the last of the apostles, besides Paul, the great apostle to the Gentiles, so far as can be learned from the record, were favored with post-ascension epiphanies of our Lord. But from the heavenly glory, Paul had numerous "visions and revelations of the Lord." It was by a personal appearance of the glorified Christ, that Paul was converted, appointed to apostleship, and instructed and equipped for his work. It was by special, supernatural revelations of

Christ from heaven to him, and not otherwise, that Paul was effectually instructed in the entire system of Christianity, which he was called to teach and establish. In this extraordinary way, Paul became versed not only in the facts, doctrines, ethics, and institutions of the gospel, but also in the distinctive characteristics and mutual relations of the old and new dispensations, and in the practical bearings of the gospel to both Gentiles and Jews. The revelation thus made directly by Christ to Paul was full and final, and it needed not to be supplemented from any earthly source or supervised by any earthly authority. Paul solemnly asserts that he received his gospel neither from other apostles, nor from private Christians, nor from any man or men whatsoever; and declares that he is "an apostle (not from man, neither through man, but through Jesus Christ and

God the Father, who raised him from the dead.)"[a] Again he asseverates, "For I make known to you, brethren, as touching the gospel which was preached by me, that it is not after man. For neither did I receive it from man, nor was I taught it, but it came to me through the revelation of Jesus Christ."[b] Further he avers, "By revelation was made known unto me the mystery .... which in other generations was not made known unto the sons of men, as it hath now been revealed unto his holy apostles and prophets in the Spirit; to wit, that the Gentiles are fellow-heirs and fellow-members of the body and fellow-partakers of the promise in Christ Jesus through the gospel."[c] Not only did Paul receive the entire gospel exclusively from the ascended Christ himself personally, but the very terms in which, by divine inspiration, he ex-

[a] Gal. 1: 1.   [b] Gal. 1: 11, 12.   [c] Eph. 3: 3, 5, 6.

pressed it, he knew to be "the word of God," as he emphatically declares in what is generally acknowledged to be the first written of all his Epistles: "And for this cause we also thank God without ceasing, that, when ye received from us the word of the message, even the word of God, ye accepted it not as the word of men, but, as it is in truth, the word of God."[a]

It is in view of his absolute certainty of the divine source from which, and the infallible way in which, he received the gospel, and in view of the efficient manner in which, through the Holy Spirit, he made it known, and gave it miraculous certification, that he so sternly anathematizes those Judaizing teachers, who would "pervert the gospel of Christ," as received and delivered by him: "Though we, or an angel from heaven, should preach unto you any gospel other than that

[a] 1 Thess. 2: 13.

which we preached unto you, let him be anathema. As we have said before, so say I now again, If any man preacheth unto you any gospel other than that which ye received let him be anathema." [a]

As soon as he was commissioned and instructed by revelation of the glorified Christ, he set about his apostolic work at once, without consulting the other apostles, or any of them. On this point, he says distinctly, "But when it was the good pleasure of God, who separated me from my mother's womb, and called me through his grace, to reveal his Son in me, that I might preach him among the Gentiles; immediately I conferred not with flesh and blood: neither went I up to Jerusalem to them which were apostles before me: but I went into Arabia; and again I returned unto Damascus. Then after three years I

[a] Gal. 1: 8, 9.

went up to Jerusalem to visit Cephas and tarried with him fifteen days. But other of the apostles saw I none, save James the Lord's brother."[a] It would be at this time, three years after his conversion, that there occurred the interesting incident in the early Christian life of Paul, which is thus related by Luke: "And when he come to Jerusalem and assayed to join himself to the disciples and they were afraid of him, not believing that he was a disciple. But Barnabas took him and brought him to the apostles [Peter and James], and declared unto them how he had seen the Lord in the way, and that he had spoken to him, and how at Damascus he had preached boldly in the name of Jesus."[b]

As we learn from the Epistle to the Galatians, Paul was three years in actual and active apostleship before he saw any of the other apostles; that

[a] Gal. 1: 15-19.   [b] Acts 9: 26, 27.

even then he had only one short interview with Peter and James; and that, for a long period afterwards, he "was still unknown by face unto the churches of Judea."[a]

In the same letter, he says, further, that "fourteen years after" this brief visit, "I went up again to Jerusalem," "by revelation;" "and I laid before them the gospel which I preach among the Gentiles."[b] "But from those who were reputed to be somewhat ..... they, I say, who were of repute imparted nothing to me; but contrariwise, when they saw that I had been intrusted with the gospel of the uncircumcision, even as Peter with the gospel of the circumcision (for he that wrought for Peter unto the apostleship of the circumcision wrought for me also unto the Gentiles), and when they perceived the grace that was given unto me, James and Cephas and

[a] Gal. 1: 18–24.   [b] Gal. 2: 1, 2.

John, they who were reputed to be pillars, gave to me and Barnabas the right hand of fellowship, that we should go unto the Gentiles, and they unto the circumcision."[a]

The business on which Paul, "by revelation," went up at this time to Jerusalem was the extremely important matter relating to the liberties of Gentile Christians, for which Paul contended successfully in the apostolic council there, as described with much fullness in the fifteenth chapter of Acts.

As has been already indicated, the Epistle to the Galatians shows conclusively, and this is strongly corroborated by both Epistles to the Corinthians, that the entire gospel of Christ, and the full apostleship to proclaim it, and to establish its institutions, especially among the Gentiles, Paul received, not from man, nor through the

[a] Gal. 2: 6–9.

instrumentality of man, but directly from his ascended and self-revealed Lord. This, the other apostles acknowledged as readily and fully as he acknowledged the genuineness and divine origin of the gospel they proclaimed and the apostleship they exercised.

Besides the post-ascension appearings of Christ to him, Paul had one experience, confirmatory of his apostleship, more extraordinary, in its essential character, than any undergone by the other apostles, John in Patmos not excepted. About the year 56 of the Christian era, Paul (whether in the body or out of the body, he knew not) was "caught up into the third heaven," "caught up into Paradise," and "heard unspeakable words which it is not lawful for a man to utter,"[a] which, whatever they imported, strengthened and confirmed him in his independent

[a] 2 Cor. 12: 2-4.

and absolute apostleship. This wonderful experience, while it was followed by an abiding and humbling personal affliction, was followed also by the divine promise of grace all-sufficient for his personal and apostolic duties and trials.[a] In confirmation of his full divine inspiration and of his true apostolic message, mission, and authority, Paul was divinely invested with exceptional miraculous powers. The writer of the Acts says, "And God wrought special miracles by the hands of Paul: insomuch that unto the sick were carried away from his body handkerchiefs or aprons, and the diseases departed from them, and the evil spirits went out."[b] In writing to the Romans, Paul himself says, "I will not dare to speak of any things save those which Christ wrought through me, for the obedience of the Gentiles, by word and deed, in the power of signs and

[a] 2 Cor. 12: 8, 9.   [b] Acts 19: 11, 12.

wonders, in the power of the Holy Ghost." ᵃ In writing to the Corinthian church, among other things, concerning its abuse of its manifold supernatural gifts, especially the gift of tongues, and, indirectly, concerning the claims of his own apostleship, Paul says, "I thank God, I speak with tongues more than you all: howbeit in the church I had rather speak five words with my understanding, that I might instruct others also, than ten thousand words in a tongue." ᵇ "In nothing was I behind the very chiefest of the apostles, though I am nothing. Truly the signs of an apostle were wrought among you in all patience, by signs and wonders and mighty works." ᶜ Paul had also, in great degree, the exclusively apostolic power of conferring spiritual gifts by the laying on of hands — the gift of tongues and the gift of prophecy particularly — as recorded instances dis-

ᵃ Rom. 15: 18, 19.   ᵇ 1 Cor. 14: 18, 19.   ᶜ 2 Cor. 12: 11, 12.

tinctly show.[a] He had also, in full measure, the apostolic power of visiting summary and condign punishment on notorious and specially pernicious offenders, for the warning of others, doubtless; but, also, with a view, if it might be, of bringing the transgressors themselves to repentance. Thus speaking of the pains and penalties which he inflicted upon "Hymenæus and Alexander," by delivering them for a time, into the dread hands of the lord of all evil, because of their shipwrecking course concerning the faith, Paul says, "Whom I have delivered unto Satan, that they may be taught not to blaspheme."[b] In the exercise of this same judicial and punitive power, the apostle writes peremptorily to the Corinthian church, in relation to an exceedingly iniquitous offender in its membership: "For I

[a] Acts 19: 6. 2 Tim. 1: 6. Cf. 1 Tim. 4: 14.
[b] 1 Tim. 1: 20.

verily being absent in body but present in spirit, have already, as though I were present, judged him that hath so wrought this thing, in the name of our Lord Jesus, ye being gathered together, and my spirit, with the power of our Lord Jesus, to deliver such a one unto Satan for the destruction of the flesh, that the spirit may be saved in the day of the Lord Jesus."[a]

In both of his Epistles to the Corinthians, especially in the ninth chapter of the First Epistle and from the tenth chapter to the end of the Second Epistle, and in the first and second chapters of his Epistle to the Galatians, Paul asserts, and defends his apostolic standing and authority, with great fulness and power—driven to it, against his natural modesty, by the contentiousness and disparaging methods of the Judaizing teachers, and their consequent evil influence toward the pure gospel of Christ.

[a] 1 Cor. 5: 3–5.

In the stern rebuke which Paul administered to Peter, recorded in the Epistle to the Galatians, there is a strong illustration of Paul's independent apostleship. The ground of his censure of Peter was not any official difference of view as to gospel truth, or order, but a temporary personal and private inconsistency of conduct on the part of Peter, in relation to social intercourse between Christian Jews and Christian Gentiles—the momentary cowardice of a really courageous man, humbly trying to avoid giving offense. This, not only on account of the moral dereliction involved in it, but also because of its evil practical bearing on gospel liberty, Paul sharply, justly, and withal, fraternally, rebukes. A few years afterward, Peter in his Second Epistle, declares, in humble brotherly fashion, that "our beloved brother Paul" wrote "in all his Epistles," "according to the wisdom given unto him," and that Paul's words thus written are "Scripture."^a To Peter's mind, "Scripture" was "the word of God;" and, to Peter's knowledge, Peter's Master had said, "The Scripture cannot be broken."^b So the Apostle Peter's testimony corroborates the apostolic claim of Paul that the things which he wrote "are the commandment of the Lord."^c

The seeming contradiction between the teaching of Paul and that of James, on the doctrine of justification, affords no ground for disparagement of the divine authority of either Paul or James; for the difference between them is merely apparent, and not real, as a careful examination of their writings on the subject, considered from the proper points of view, would plainly show. In no degree, and in no sense, are they either opposing, or even referring to, each other's views.

^a 2 Peter 2: 15, 16.   ^b John 10: 35.   ^c 1 Cor. 14: 37.

Each is contending with a different antagonist — Paul with the Christless legalist; James with the lawless antinomian. Each is treating of a different sort of faith — Paul commending an evangelical, living, fruitful faith; James impugning a barely intellectual, unevangelical, and wholly barren faith. Each is speaking of a different kind of works — Paul showing the worthlessness of unevangelical, legal, dead works; James showing the value and acceptableness of evangelical, and, therefore, really good works, and their usefulness as evidence of genuine faith. Each is discussing different aspects, if not different kinds, of justification — Paul the justification of the soul by faith, before God; James the justification of the believer's profession of faith by his works, before men: and so, also, each, by way of illustration, is referring to entirely different incidents and periods in the life of Abraham — Paul to the faith of Abraham at the outset of his believing career, which was counted unto him for righteousness; James to the obedience of Abraham in an incident of his life twenty years later, which justified, or proved, Abraham to all men as a true believer. Each is governed by a different purpose — Paul is endeavoring to set right the man who is building on a false foundation; James is endeavoring to induce indolent and inconsistent professors to build the right superstructure. Paul endeavors to plant the right root; James to develop the right fruit. Paul endeavors to lead his readers to attain true justification; James, to give true evidence of their justification.

Nearly any two evangelical men contending, respectively, with legalists and antinomians, and almost any one and the same person contending with those opposite errors alternately, would be sure, especially if their arguments were glanced at unreflectingly, to show the same apparent, but unreal, contrarieties of doctrine, while in reality their teachings, like those of Paul and James, would be, uninterruptedly, in the profoundest harmony. These two apostles, like two friendly swordsmen standing back to back in the midst of their enemies, in reality, defend each other, while each is contending with a different foe.

From every point of view, the proofs of the genuineness of Paul's apostleship are ample and convincing.

Chapter IV.

THE EXTRAORDINARY CHARACTER OF PAUL'S APOSTOLIC MISSION.

The mission of the twelve apostles, appointed early in the earthly ministry of our Lord, was to plant living Christianity in the heart of dead and decaying Judaism. Their humble origin, their provincial birth and rearing, their scanty culture and even their strong and narrow Jewish prejudices, so far from being hindrances to their work, were in reality, conditions and factors of their success. A broader culture, a more cosmopolitan spirit, would have been prejudicial to their apostolic mission among the Jews resident in Judea and Galilee; for then, they would have aroused against themselves and their cause, the spirit of prejudice, intolerance, and deadly hostility. Their mission, like the earthly mission of their Lord, was chiefly Jewish in its immediate aims and bearings. They were chosen as official witnesses of the entire public ministry of Christ, which, with the exception of two brief incidents, was wholly among the Jewish people in Judea and Galilee; and thus, also, Matthias was chosen, probably from among "the seventy," in the place of the lost Judas.

The Christianity implanted by "the twelve," in the midst of the Judaism of Palestine, while in nature distinct from it, as the mistletoe from the decaying oak in which it is rooted, was never completely disentangled by them from the roots and offshoots of Judaism.

As a consequence, though not endorsed by "the twelve," the Christianity of their Jewish converts was apt to have a decidedly Judaistic flavor;

and their converts in Jerusalem and Judea were inclined to have an instinctive and strong Judaistic tendency. The Jewish Christianity thus developed under "the twelve," who themselves had been singularly slow to learn Christ's will concerning the gospel call and reception of the Gentiles, was of such a type that their Jewish disciples were strongly disposed and, indeed, obstinately determined, to Judaize the Gentiles before Christianizing them; to demand their submission to rites and ceremonies of the Jewish ceremonial law, which Christ's death had fulfilled and rendered obsolete, before admitting them to the privileges of the gospel—as if Christians were merely a Jewish sect, loftier and more advanced than older ones then existing, but requiring that a Gentile must become ceremonially and practically a Jew, in order to be admitted into it. Though this characteristic trend was not brought about, or countenanced, by "the twelve," neither was it effectually counteracted by them. Indeed, the Judaizing tendency of the Jewish disciples of "the twelve," though without their apostolic warrant, and notwithstanding the explicit decision against it, by the apostolic council at Jerusalem, continued from its inception, through all after-times, to be, in all Christendom, a pernicious, insinuating, and aggressive evil.

The characteristics and limitations which helped to qualify "the twelve" for the work of Christianizing their compatriots in their native land unfitted them, largely, for a length of time, for aggressive work in the Christianization of the Gentiles, notwithstanding the fact that under a divine compulsion, Peter, in the case of Cornelius and his household, opened the door of Christianity to the Gentiles, and notwithstanding the fact that, in their later years and in other lands, Peter and John and other apostles seem to have worked almost indiscriminately among Jews and Gentiles. The work of "the twelve" was primarily and pre-eminently a gospel mission to "the twelve tribes"— or what was left of them—scattered everywhere; for which they were thoroughly qualified, and in which, as we may infer from the early portion of the Acts, from the testimony of Paul, especially in his Galatian and Corinthian Epistles, and from the general Epistles of Peter, John, and James, they were eminently successful.

But the "other sheep," who were not of Christ's Jewish "fold,"[a] of whom Christ prophetically spoke and concerning whom he greatly rejoiced in spirit, could be gathered and brought in, fully and effectually, only by another — a more largely, variously, and specially gifted and equipped — kind of apostolic shepherd.

[a] John 10: 16.

The peculiar and extraordinary task of introducing and organizing Christianity, free from Judaistic taint and tendency, on the enlarged basis of an additional, new, and independent revelation of Christ and his will, was reserved for one who, by reason of his unequalled natural endowments; his great attainments in Hebrew Scripture and Jewish ceremonialism; his intimate knowledge of pagan literatures, philosophies and religions; his Hellenistic birth and rearing; his Roman citizenship and knowledge of the world; his dialectic and oratorical skill; and, above all, his miraculous conversion, his personal meetings with the ascended Lord, his instruction through personal revelations of Christ, his special appointment by Christ, to apostleship, his own special Pentecostal experience in the Spirit, and his vast and varied supernatural knowledge and powers, was qualified to be at once the Moses and the Joshua of the new dispensation.

No one of "the twelve," nor all of them put together, had a tithe of his preparation and fitness for his peculiar task of severing and launching the life-boat of Christianity from the sinking hulk of Judaism; of confronting on their own ground, and overpowering, the demons of paganism; and, while recognizing and extracting the few shrivelled grains of truth then existing in Judaism, and the much fewer and feebler grains of truth then existing in paganism, broadly and thoroughly implanting and developing Christianity untainted with the poison, and untinged with the hue, of either paganism or Judaism, in the great centres and outlying regions of Europe and Asia. How zealously, extensively, uncompromisingly, and thoroughly, he accomplished the mighty undertaking, the sacred record abundantly shows. His imperial apostolic influence has ever been present and predominant wherever Christianity has obtained a foothold in the world. Manifestly, also, he steadfastly regarded Christianity, in its true light, as a universal and uncompromising religion; and he constantly aimed at the fraternal unification of Jews and Gentiles under its banner of light and love.

Though ready and eager to make the first offer of Christ and his salvation to the Jewish people, wherever he met them in the Gentile world, still his mission was essentially and supremely a mission to the Gentiles. Immediately after his conversion, the Lord said concerning him, "He is a chosen vessel unto me to bear my name unto the Gentiles and Kings, and the children of Israel."[a] In writing to the Christians in Rome, Paul

[a] Acts 9: 15.

says, "Inasmuch then as I am an apostle of Gentiles, I glorify my ministry;"[a] and, in writing to Timothy, he says, "I was appointed a preacher and an apostle (I speak the truth, I lie not), a teacher of the Gentiles in faith and truth."[b]

While neither conflict, nor discrimination, may be admitted between the apostles of Christ as to the authority of their apostolic acts and writings, it must be borne in mind that Paul is peculiarly and pre-eminently the apostle to the Gentiles; that, by Christ himself, he was specially called and commissioned to the Gentile apostleship; and that Paul's writings contain the fullest and most advanced revelation of Christ's will — a revelation of Christ's will which, while absolutely binding on both Jews and Gentiles, has, nevertheless, a peculiar breadth and fitness of application to the cir-

[a] Rom. 11: 13.   [b] 1 Tim. 2: 7.

cumstances and needs of the Gentile races. It was peculiarly his office to determine and "teach" the truths, "set in order" the institutions, and "ordain" the order, of the Christian system, among the Gentiles; and the things, therefore, which he wrote are forever to be received as "the commandment of the Lord." So far, therefore, from discriminating against, or disparaging, or ignoring, the apostolic authority of Paul, we, as Gentile peoples, should give special heed to his writings, as divinely designed for us in particular.

CHAPTER V.

THE APOSTOLICITY OF PAUL'S WRITINGS.

The apostolic letters naturally succeeded the other work of the apostles; and they were needed to supplement, confirm, and perpetuate it. In the earlier stages of their heaven-appointed business, the work of converting sinners to Christ, of organizing believers into churches, and of instructing them in the truths and principles of Chrisianity, could effectually be done only by their word of mouth and personal activity. But when exercising their apostolic supervision and control of the many widely separated churches, apostolic writing became a necessity. The oral teachings of the apostles would be in the greatest danger of mutilation and distortion, from popular forgetfulness and the inevitable aberrations of tradition; and so, for the full and perfect preservation of their teachings in their own time, and much more necessarily in all aftertimes, they were obliged to have recourse to the abiding instrumentality, and minute accuracy of parchment, pen, and ink. The vagaries, uncertainties, and contradictions of tradition, in ages before and after apostolic times, demonstrate its futility as a medium of permanent divine revelation. The safety of the Christian revelation could be secured only by inspired writings.

The authority and impulse to write, and the matter and form of the writing, in the case both of prophets and of apostles, were of divine origin. Moses "wrote" "by the commandment of the Lord;"[a] for, "the Lord said unto Moses, Write this for a memorial in a

[a] Num. 33: 2.

book;"ᵃ and what he wrote was called "the book of the law of Moses, which the Lord had commanded to Israel,"ᵇ "the words of the God of Israel."ᶜ Speaking through Hosea, concerning Ephraim, God said, "Though I write for him my law in ten thousand precepts, they are counted as a strange thing."ᵈ To Jeremiah, the divine command to write came peremptorily, "Take thee a roll of a book, and write therein all the words that I have spoken unto thee."ᵉ In the divine communication of the Apocalypse, the Apostle John many times received the command to "write;" and he appends to this marvellous writing the most solemn and terrible warning against adding to, or taking from, "the words of the book of this prophecy."ᶠ The apostolic and divine design of his gospel he thus stated: "These [things]

ᵃ Ex. 17: 14.   ᵇ Neh. 8: 1.   ᶜ Ezra 9: 4.
ᵈ Hos. 8: 12.   ᵉ Jer. 36: 1.   ᶠ Rev. 22: 19.

are written, that ye may believe that Jesus is the Christ, the Son of God; and that believing ye may have life in his name."ᵃ Peter writes, as an "apostle of Jesus Christ," concerning the things of the gospel, as he tells us, in order "that at every time ye may be able after my decease to call these things to remembrance;"ᵇ and, as we have already seen, he declares that Paul, "in all his epistles," wrote, "according to the wisdom given to him," and, impliedly, places Paul's writings on the same level of divine inspiration and authority as that of "the other scriptures."ᶜ Paul himself declares that in writing he has "the mind of Christ" and "the Spirit of God;" and that what he writes is "the commandment of the Lord."

Concerning the divine origin of his gospel teaching, and of the language

ᵃ John 20: 31. Cf. 1 John 1: 1–4. ᵇ 2 Peter 1: 1, 15.
ᶜ 2 Peter 3: 15, 16

in which it was couched, whether written or spoken, Paul says, "which things also we speak, not in words which man's wisdom teacheth, but which the Spirit teacheth"[a]—a statement which at a single stroke shatters the shallow and foolish theory of inspiration which maintains that while the thoughts of the apostles concerning the gospel were divinely imparted, their words were left purely to their unaided, undirected choice—a theory which ignores the radical distinction between revelation and inspiration, and which, in effect, acknowledges and discerns no inspiration at all.

By the Divine Spirit that possessed them, the apostles, Matthew, Peter, John, and Paul, were driven to write, in order that the divine revelations made to them might not become fugitive and evanescent, but abiding and available for all time.

[a] 1 Cor. 2: 13.

The writings of Paul and of the other apostles, though epistolary in form, were not private and temporary communications, but were of general and permanent character. Indeed, the epistolary form was better adapted for free, familiar, fraternal, yet authoritative, communication of advanced Christian truth having multiplicity of practical bearings, to redeemed, regenerate brethren inside the church of Christ, than the more formal, oracular style of composition, anciently employed by the prophets, toward the unbelieving, carnal Jewish nation and the impenitent, hostile world without. It was a discriminating remark of Bengel, that "The epistolary form is a pre-eminence of the Scriptures of the New Testament as compared with those of the Old."

The Pauline Epistles naturally arrange themselves into several significant groups, which suggestively present Paul's conception of the nature and work of apostleship, from various points of view. First come the First and Second Letters to the Thessalonians; then the Letters to the Romans, Corinthians and Galatians, which resemble one another in matter and aim; then the letters of the first imprisonment — Ephesians, Philippians, Colossians, and Philemon; then the pastoral Epistles to Timothy and Titus. Hebrews, whatever its relation to Paul, stands by itself. The careful study of these different groups of Pauline letters, growing out of various periods, circumstances, and experiences, and showing the full supply of the Spirit granted him for every apostolic situation and need, demonstrate strikingly the great range, power, and authority of Paul's function as an apostle.

In nine of the thirteen or fourteen Epistles ascribed to him — leaving undetermined the Pauline authorship of Hebrews — Paul distinctly asserts, in the opening sentences, his apostleship, to remind his readers of the apostolic character, purpose, and authority of his letters; and in all his Epistles alike, he exercises supreme apostolic authority. From the outset onward he was careful to secure, by his sign manual and style of handwriting, the identification of his apostolic letters, and to guard them from being fraudulently, or mistakenly, confounded with the writings of any other person, as is indicated by a letter belonging to the first group of his Epistles: "The salutation of me Paul with mine own hand, which is the token in every epistle: so I write."[a]

Professedly, or impliedly, the letters of Paul are apostolic in design and force; and, in them, he exercises the widest and most absolute author-

[a] 2 Thess. 3: 17.

ity. In Second Thessalonians he says, "We have confidence in the Lord touching you, that ye both do and will do the things which we command."[a] "Now we command you, brethren, in the name of our Lord Jesus Christ, that ye withdraw yourselves from every brother that walketh disorderly, and not after the tradition which they received of us."[b] Writing to the Corinthian church, and giving specific commands, he says, "And so ordain I in all the churches:"[c] "If any man thinketh himself to be a prophet, or spiritual, let him take knowledge of the things which I write unto you, that they are the commandment of the Lord:"[d] "Now concerning the collection for the saints, as I gave order to the churches of Galatia, so also do ye."[e] Writing to the Colossians, he makes reference to

---

[a] 2 Thess. 3: 4.   [b] 2 Thess. 3: 6.   [c] 1 Cor. 7: 17.
[d] 1 Cor. 14: 37.   [e] 1 Cor. 16: 1.

"Mark, the cousin of Barnabas," and says, "touching whom ye received commandments; if he come unto you, receive him."[a] Writing to Timothy concerning the management of the meetings of the churches, he says, "But I permit not a woman to teach, nor to have dominion over a man, but to be in quietness."[b]

Such is the tone of unlimited, unqualified authority, which — often in harmonious combination with tones of tearful remonstrance and tender entreaty — pervades all the writings of the Apostle Paul, concerning every matter of Christian faith and duty, in individual, social, or churchly life.

The function, therefore, of Paul's writings is clearly, strongly apostolic. They treat authoritatively of Christianity abstract and applied, and cover the whole range of Christian thought, feeling, and action. Like the other

[a] Col. 4: 10.   [b] 1 Tim. 2: 12.

apostolic Epistles, they are an advance upon the teaching of the four Gospels and of the Acts. In the Gospels, we have presented to us the nature, character, work, and aims of Christ, as manifested in the facts of his earthly life, ministry, sufferings, death, and resurrection. In the Acts, we see Christ, the facts pertaining to him, and the salvation procured by him, proclaimed by apostles, and other preachers, to the world; the organization of those who believed, into churches; and the beginnings of church life and activity. But the Epistles are, in fact, if not in form, inspired interpretations and expositions of the Gospels and the Acts; and, besides that, they are divinely inspired communications of larger, and more minutely applied, revelations of Christian truth and duty — all made, not to the outer unbelieving world; but to, and within, the churchly circles of believers. Paul's letters are an authoritative enlargement and exposition of the revelation of God's truth and will. In these letters, Paul apostolically adjudicates upon all manner of questions, doctrinal, experimental, and practical; and though in many instances the immediate occasions of his discussions may have passed away forever, yet the truths and principles which he reveals, and sets forth, are of everlasting validity and of universal application. Like Hale's "Analysis," Blackstone's "Commentaries," and Coke on Littleton—elucidations of the meaning and applications of law, which have the force of law themselves—Paul's letters, while giving us Christianity expanded, give us, also, Christianity authoritatively expounded and applied. Paul's recorded decisions on the many major and minor questions, of various kinds, that came before him for settlement, are inspired precedents, for the decision of numberless analogous questions of all sorts, in all ages, to the end of time. Thus it comes to pass, that much of our Christian knowledge, many of our distinctively Christian principles, and most of our Christian methods of procedure, in every department of Christian life and labor, are divinely given us, through the Epistles of Paul. Besides unfolding, in these letters, the great mass of Christian truth and duty in general, he, as peculiarly the apostle to the Gentiles, particularly makes known the mystery of their call to the full privileges of the gospel; defends their freedom from the yoke of Jewish ceremonialism; and sheds the fullest light on the entire gospel of Christ, in its relations to the Gentile world. These Epistles being, in their entire contents, a perfect revelation of the mind of Christ, given through the inspiration of the Spirit of God, are all, and every part of them, of supreme authority, on all subjects of which they treat, and to which they apply.

The particular Epistle from which the theme of this work is mainly derived — the First Epistle to the Corinthians — is very varied in its topics, and exceedingly rich and fruitful in its treatment of them. Principles of lofty character, and far-reaching applicability and importance, are developed in it, often in a casual way, while the apostle answers questions of local or general, and temporary or permanent significance — concerning the use of meats offered to idols, concerning celibacy, marriage, and divorce, and concerning the use of spiritual gifts in public religious exercises. From these apostolic decisions there is no appeal; and the principles apostolically laid down are of everlasting validity.

Strangely enough, there are not a few persons, who, misapprehending Paul's meaning in three closely connected passages in his First Epistle to the Corinthians, and not observing the drift of the argument of which these passages are links, imagine that while parts of Paul's Epistles are inspired, other parts of them are uninspired; and they maintain that Paul himself so teaches in these brief, succinct portions of the Epistle.

Now suppose, merely for argument's sake, that Paul is there admitting the non-inspiration of these same parts of this Epistle, then it follows that he knows when he is inspired, and when not; and that, in the latter case, he is, as in duty bound, careful to point out when his non-inspiration occurs; and as there is no other such passage in any of his Epistles, it follows that, with the exception of these few, brief, plainly indicated sentences, forming a small part of one chapter of one Epistle, all Paul's writings are fully inspired.

But it can readily be shown that these passages bear no such meaning, make no such reference, and warrant no such inference; and that, on the contrary, they necessarily involve the highest claims to apostolic inspiration and authority, and are, themselves, the strongest exercise of these divine gifts. These short, interwoven parts of the Epistle were the apostle's replies to queries addressed to him by the Corinthian church, relative to marriage, in a time of great persecution and general disturbance, when the Jewish nation was about to be broken up, and the near approach of the end of all things, foreshadowed by that event, was commonly apprehended. In this time of disquietude and unrest, there were those who doubted whether the marriage bond and relationship, even when both parties were Christians, should be maintained; who questioned more especially whether mixed marriages already existing between Christians and their heathen husbands or wives should not be promptly dissolved; and, further, who had grave apprehensions as to whether there was not grievous sin in making, or in aiding and abetting the making of, marriage contracts, even in the case of virgins, in such perilous circumstances, and in the face of such approaching events and disasters. To these three questions the apostle definitely replied.

Now, the whole mistake, so frequently made concerning the passages which contain his replies, consists in gratuitously supposing that, in them, Paul is contrasting the utterances of Paul uninspired with the utterances of Paul inspired, instead of recognizing that Paul is, on the one hand, quoting the sayings of Christ, uttered when he was personally on the earth, or when speaking through the Old Testament prophets, and, on the other hand, stating his own Spirit-guided decisions, as Christ's fully inspired, fully accredited apostle. In thus putting his apostolic decisions side by side with the mandates of Christ on earth, Paul makes the authority of both unquestionable. In the one case, Christ was speaking with his own personal human lips; in the other, Christ was speaking in and through his inspired apostle.

There had been divine commands concerning marriage in the laws of Moses, in the utterances of the prophets, and in the sayings of our Lord during his earthly ministry. These commands covered some, but not all, of the questions relative to marriage, which constantly arose in mixed communities, and among heathen converts to Christianity, in apostolic times.

The first of the three Pauline passages referred to relates to the question of divorce of Christian husbands and wives, and reads thus: "But unto the married I give charge, yea not I, but the Lord, That the wife depart not from her husband (but and if she depart, let her remain unmarried, or else be reconciled to her husband); and that the husband leave not his wife."[a] In the days of his flesh, our Lord had spoken distinctly and emphatically enough, forbidding all such separations: "So that they are no more twain, but one flesh. What therefore God hath joined together, let not man put asunder."[b] "And I say unto you, Whosoever shall put away his wife, except for fornication, and shall marry another, committeth adultery: and he that marrieth her when she is put away committeth

[a] 1 Cor. 7: 10
[b] Matt. 19: 6. Cf. Mal 2: 14-16

adultery."[a] This being the Lord's own personal command during his life on earth, Paul simply repeats it: "But to the married I give charge, yea not I, but the Lord, That the wife depart not from her husband . . . . and that the husband leave not his wife."[b] When a true law exists that fully covers the class of cases for which it was enacted, why make another law in its stead? Had the Lord himself not already given a command concerning the matter, Paul, as his inspired apostle, would have been prepared infallibly to decide the case, but the Lord, while on earth, having spoken, Paul simply echoes and emphasizes his command.

The second passage occurs only two verses further on, and relates to the dissolution of mixed marriages then existing between Christians and the heathen. The divine commands by the prophets under the legal Jewish

[a] Matt. 19: 9.   [b] 1 Cor. 7: 10.

dispensation forbade marriages of God's ancient people with the heathen, and required the putting away of heathen wives;ª but in his earthly life and ministry among the unmixed Jewish people in Judea and Galilee, the Lord himself said nothing bearing directly on the question, which in the circumstances did not come up, and needed not then to be discussed. But now that, in entirely changed surroundings, the question had arisen in mixed communities and pressed itself to the front, Paul, with the fullest divine inspiration, as Christ's apostle to the Gentiles, gives his positive, authoritative decision, supplementing previous revelations of Christ's will and annulling Israel's ancient prophetic law, so far as it might be thought to have any bearing on the case. Here is his apostolic decree: "But to the rest say I, not the Lord: If any brother

---

ª See Deut. 7: 3; 1 Kings 11: 2; Ezra 10: 3.

hath an unbelieving wife, and she is content to dwell with him, let him not leave her. And the woman which hath an unbelieving husband, and he is content to dwell with her, let her not leave her husband."[a] Nothing but the fullest consciousness of being possessed of Christ's mind, and of being the mouthpiece of the Holy Spirit, could have warranted him in making and enforcing such a decision. Nowhere else does he exercise higher apostolic authority, or imply the possession of ampler divine inspiration.

The third and last of these passages occurs thirteen verses still further on, though it is virtually the resumption of a subject started in the first part of the same chapter; and it relates to the question whether it was not utterly wrong, in the circumstances, for virgins to marry, or be given in marriage; concerning which matter, many

[a] 1 Cor. 7: 12.

Christians were in painful doubt. On this point, Paul gives no command whatever — the Lord had given none while on earth, neither does he give any now by his apostle. On the contrary, Paul apostolically declares that there was no sin, even at that time, either in marrying, or in giving in marriage; either in refraining from marrying, or in restraining from marrying. It was not a question of right and wrong, but of personal expediency and private judgment. But though Paul gives no command in relation to this question, he, nevertheless, gives his apostolic judgment, or advice, that, owing to the troublous times, then existing, and still further apprehended in the near future, or "the present distress," as he calls it, it would be better, on the score of greater freedom from trouble and greater liberty for Christian service, to remain single. As one who has obtained "the grace," the "mercy," of full, inspired apostleship, in which to be faithful, as a steward of the mysteries of the kingdom, in resolving all such doubts and cases of conscience, for the people of God, he gives his apostolic judgment, or advice. It was part of this apostolic counsel that, in this particular matter, each person should feel himself at liberty to act in accordance with his private estimate of his individual nature and circumstances. The passage runs thus: "Now concerning virgins I have no commandment of the Lord: but I give my judgment, as one that hath obtained mercy of the Lord to be faithful. I think therefore that this is good by reason of the present distress, namely, that it is good for a man to be as he is. . . . . But and if thou marry, thou hast not sinned; and if a virgin marry she hath not sinned. Yet such shall have tribulation in the flesh: and I would spare you."[a]

To sum the matter up:— In the first of the three passages considered, Paul gives no apostolic command, because Christ in his earthly lifetime had given one already. In the second passage, Paul gives a full, firm apostolic command, for the reason that Christ while on earth had given none bearing upon the case. In the third passage, there is no commandment of the Lord given, one way or the other; for right and wrong were not involved in this case; and while apostolic advice is here given, part of it is, that, in this matter, private judgment of one's own case should be used in determining the course to pursue.

It is utterly irrelevant, absurd, and a sheer wresting of Scripture to interpret these passages as if, in the slightest degree, they impaired, or impugned

[a] 1 Cor. 7: 25, 26, 28.

the apostolic function and authority of any part of Paul's writings.

A few verses later on, however, referring to the same general question, there is another Pauline passage, that is sometimes spoken of as seeming to imply, upon Paul's part, a doubt of his inspiration at that particular point in the discussion: "And I think that I also have the Spirit of God."[a] In the Authorized Version, the meaning is much obscured; but in the Revised Version, as just quoted, it is brought out more clearly. The apostle is not here expressing doubt, but certainty, of his inspiration. The term he uses for "think" (δοκῶ) does not imply doubt; but, often, as in the Saviour's words, "Ye think that in them ye have eternal life,"[b] expresses firm conviction. To regard it as implying doubt, after the manner of the modern colloquial use of the English word "think," is to

[a] 1 Cor. 7: 40.   [b] John 5: 29.

mistake the idiom and usage of the Greek. Hear what the discriminating and candid Alford has to say upon the passage: "This is modestly said, implying more than is expressed by it,— not as if there were any uncertainty in his mind. It gives us the true meaning of the saying, that he is *giving his opinion*, as in verse 25: viz., not that he is speaking without inspiration, but that in the consciousness of inspiration he is giving that counsel that should determine the question." And so, substantially, say leading interpreters generally.

The words, "I also," of the passage —the "I" being emphatic—seem to glance at the pretensions of certain others, which, by strong implication, strengthens the view that, then and there, Paul felt, and, in the passage before us, was declaring, the certainty of his divine inspiration.

As, in the scheme of divine providence, the most massive and the minutest things—sidereal worlds and the motes in the sunbeam—are all, necessarily and equally, under divine inspection and control; so, in the scheme of divine inspiration, the most minute matters—such as Paul's epistolary request for his cloak, his books, and his parchments—and the most massive truths—such as the incarnation, the atonement, and the election of grace—are all, equally, under the infallible guidance and government of the inspiring Spirit of God.

RECAPITULATION.

In the progress of our argument, hitherto, we have seen the divine authority of Paul's writings to be firmly established upon four adequate basal truths: first, the nature of the apostolic office—an infallible speakership and vicegerency for Christ; secondly, the genuineness of Paul's apostleship — certified by the manifestation of all "the signs of an apostle," in him; thirdly, the extraordinary character of Paul's apostolic mission — through full and independent divine revelation and inspiration, to institute and extend pure Christianity in the Gentile world; and, fourthly, the apostolicity of Paul's writings — each and every part of them being apostolic in character and function, and, therefore, divinely inspired, and "the commandment of the Lord."

The practical bearings of the deduction, thus securely drawn, are manifold and important. To discuss them exhaustively would be impossible in a single treatise; but several of the most important of them may be outlined in the following chapters.

PART TWO.
PRACTICAL BEARINGS.

CHAPTER VI.
PRACTICAL BEARING ON EARLY CHRISTIAN HISTORY.

The epistolary correspondence of the great personages, the principal actors, and the attentive observers of any period, country, or movement, is the most important, trustworthy, and available source of history.

The transparency of purpose, the variety of topics, and the multiplicity of undesigned coincidences, characteristic of letter-writing, are the chief secrets of its historical value. The letters of Paul, when compared with each other, with Luke's account of

Paul and other apostles in Acts, and with contemporary Jewish and pagan writers, furnish, incidentally, but effectively, even apart from their inspired character, a great mass of evidence as to their own genuineness and minute accuracy; as to the truth of the gospel narrative; as to the main facts concerning the other leading apostles; and as to the historical character and course of Christianity in the first century. All this, such works as Paley's "Horæ Paulinæ," Lardner's "Credibility," and Conybeare and Howson's "Life and Epistles of St. Paul" abundantly illustrate and confirm. But the inspiration, apostolicity, and, therefore, divine authority of these letters, being firmly established, we are not left to mere conjecture, or remote inference, as to the type and course of the Christianity of the first century — that is, the formative, and perpetually authoritative type of true Christianity.

We have the nature of that Christianity defined; its spirit interpreted; its purpose unfolded; its history revealed, with absolute truth and certainty. Without the apostolic letters of Paul, our knowledge of the early history of Christianity would be of the most meagre and unsatisfactory description. With them, primitive and apostolic Christian history is accessible, well defined, and easily within our mental grasp.

Chapter VII.
PRACTICAL BEARING ON CHRISTIAN DOCTRINE.

All teaching is based on fact. The rationale of fact is the substance of doctrine. Christian doctrine is based upon, and grows out of, the historical facts of the New Testament—the facts relating to the personal Christ, and those relating to his apostles, officially considered.

Of the vast body of Christian truth thus revealed in the New Testament, concerning God and man, law and gospel, this world and the next, a great part is attributable to the writings of Paul. For the sake of brevity, cursory mention of a few characteristic Pauline doctrines must suffice for these pages; and Paul's teaching concerning the unity and tri-personality of God, the union of the divine and human natures in Christ, may safely be assumed without discussion.

The doctrine of vicarious and imputed righteousness is one of the most characteristic of Paul's teachings. After proving that God, through his law natural and revealed, requires righteousness from all men, that all men are in fact destitute of righteousness, and that, for lack of righteousness, or for positive unrighteousness, all men are under legal condemnation, the apostle shows that Christ, by his obedient life and sacrificial death, offered freely to God in our behalf, has fulfilled the precept and exhausted the penalty of the law, and that thus he has brought in an infinite, everlasting, and substitutionary righteousness; so that, as to righteousness, he becomes the end of the law, and the hope of the gospel, to every one who believes in him.

Of the election of divine grace, to a full and inalienable interest in the vicarious work of Christ, and to all consequent blessings, regeneration, faith and final salvation included—though that truth is distinctly asserted by Christ himself, by Luke, and by Peter—Paul treats with great fulness and power, maintaining that the election to salvation is divine, gratuitous, personal, inalienable, eternal.

Justification by faith, while unquestionably present and potent in the other New Testament writings, is preeminently a Pauline doctrine; and our apostle declares, proves, defines, illustrates and enforces it, with great energy, and fertility of resource; and has made it the keystone of the arch of Christian truth, and the key of the ark of salvation.

The spiritual union of Christ and believers, a truth rooted in Christ's own personal teachings, is taught by Paul, with vast weight of argument, and with great wealth of metaphor and illustration.

Paul's discussion of the doctrine of the resurrection of the body, has, toward the close of his First Letter to the Corinthians, particularly, a singular breadth of view, a resistless sweep of argumentation, and the swell and ring of a prophetic poem and pæan of victory.

On these and many other Christian doctrines, Paul's teaching is full, explicit, authoritative, final; and in relation to each and all of them, it is the province of reason, after discovering that God infallibly speaks to us through him, simply to inquire, not what he should say, but what he actually does say, and to receive it with the meekness of submission and the obedience of faith.*

* For a discussion of a group of characteristic Pauline doctrines, see Appendix I.

Chapter VIII.
Practical Bearing on Christian Ethics.

As doctrine is founded on fact or history; so ethics is founded on doctrine. Christian ethics is rooted in Christian truth; and Christian faith determines Christian duty. Christian ethics presupposes Christian dogmatics; and Christian doctrine is the means of which Christian ethics is the end. Accordingly, we find that Paul's method, in his Epistles, is to make the first two-thirds of each of them, on an average, solid doctrinal foundation; and the remaining third, firm ethical superstructure. The ethics of Paul's Epistles has an exceedingly wide range, embracing, as it does, in a distinctively Christian way, the duties of individual, domestic, social, business, civic, and churchly life.

The motives employed in distinctively Christian ethics are unique, lofty, and powerfully constraining in kind, being drawn chiefly from the character and cross of Christ; and, through the medium of the living and active word of God, they are effectually applied by the Spirit of grace. Nowhere in Scripture, are Christian motives more elevated in character, more ample in volume, or more intense in application, than they are in the writings of Paul.

In his marvellously beautiful prose poem on Christian Love — the thirteenth chapter of First Corinthians — the great apostle brings that most noble, generous, and God-like principle powerfully to bear upon the entire structure of Christian character, and upon all the relations and affairs of human life. One of the strongest applications and exemplifications of Christian love is the Pauline ethical principle of Christian expediency. This ethical principle differs radically, from commercial, political and Jesuitical expediency, in that it consists in the loving sacrifice of one's own personal rights and privileges, when needful for the safety and best interests of others, and in that it refuses to sacrifice moral for material considerations, public faith for private or party gains, or to employ evil means for the attainment of even the most worthy ends.

The writings of Paul unquestionably add fulness, elevation, applicability, and force to the system of Christian ethics.

Chapter IX.

Practical Bearing on Church Order.

Apart from the Epistles of Paul and the Acts of the Apostles—the latter written by Paul's inspired companion and helper, and largely occupied with the sayings, doings and experiences of Paul—we have extremely little in the New Testament, on the subject of church order. Among the personal utterances of Christ recorded in the Gospels, we have one strong saying from him, concerning his being personally and officially the foundation of the church universal, and another saying concerning three steps to be taken in certain cases of discipline in the church local — the brother sinned against being required privately to see the offender, and endeavor to win him to the right; that failing, he is to take with him one or two others, and with them once more attempt to win the transgressor to repentance; and should that second measure fail, the matter is to be brought before the local church, which will make final disposition of the case. This, taken from the heart of Matthew's Gospel, is practically all that the Gospels record as having been said specifically by Christ, during his earthly ministry, on the subject of the church and its order.

In the First Epistle of Peter, there is a single passage — Peter's address to the elders — which, by assigning to the elders the duties of overseer or bishop, proves the terms "bishop" and "elder" to be descriptive of one and the same office; and which, while forcibly setting forth the ministerial duties of feeding and overseeing the flock, also powerfully exhibits the duty of affectionate tractableness which the flock should exercise toward its overseers, and the humility which the members of the flock should exercise toward each other. The teaching of the Epistles of Peter on the subject of church order is almost wholly confined to this.

The letters of Jude, James, and John, while rich in nourishment for the graces of true Christian fellowship, contain almost nothing on the subject of church order.

As is evident from the transactions recorded in the earlier portion of the Book of Acts, Christ must, either personally or by his inspiring Spirit, have furnished the twelve apostles with an adequate revelation of his will on the subject of church order; but he left it for the inspired companion of Paul, while introducing his record of the greater part of Paul's apostolic ministry, to give us any knowledge of the fact.

For inspired direction on the subject of church order, we are confined, therefore, almost wholly to the Epistles of Paul, and to the Book of Acts, written by the helper of Paul, and treating largely of Paul's career.

It is with peculiar significance, therefore, that certain words of Paul bearing on this subject appeal to us: "As I gave order to the churches of Galatia, so also do ye."[a] "And so ordain I in all the churches."[b]

Section I.—The Nature of the Church.

The writings of Paul furnish an ample exposition of the nature of a New Testament church. The teachings of Paul, on this and every other subject, are in perfect accord with the teachings of all other New Testament writers; but on the subject of church order, and on almost every part of it,

[a] 1 Cor. 16: 1.   [b] 1 Cor. 7: 17.

his writings are much more varied and full than all theirs put together.

As did Christ in a single instance, so does Paul, several times, use the term "church" in what, after all, is its primary sense — the sense of the church universal; by which is meant the entire company of the finally saved, whether now in heaven or on earth, or yet to be. This, of course, is no earthly or visible organization, but a spiritual and heavenly body into which souls are directly admitted by regeneration, redemption, and adoption.

But ordinarily, Paul uses the term "church," as it is generally used in the New Testament, in the derived sense of the local, individual church; and hence, he speaks of "the church which is at Cenchrea,"[a] "the church of God which is at Corinth,"[b] "the church of the Thessalonians,"[c] "the church

[a] Rom 16:1.   [b] 1 Cor. 1:2.   [c] 1 Thess. 1:1.

which is in his house,"[a] and of "the churches of Galatia,"[b] "the churches of Macedonia,"[c] "the churches of Asia,"[d] "the churches of the Gentiles,"[e] "the churches of God."[f]

As is plainly taught in the Pauline letters, each properly constituted church of Christ is a local society, composed, exclusively, of credibly regenerated persons, duly baptized upon profession of faith in Christ, organized and conducted for Christian culture, worship, and work, and, especially, for the dissemination of Christian truth, for the keeping of the ordinances, and for the evangelization of the world.

These two significations of the term "church"—the church universal and the church local—are, properly, the only ones known to the Pauline letters, or to the New Testament. The secular

[a] Col. 4: 15. [c] 2 Cor. 8: 1.   [e] Rom. 16: 4.
[b] Gal. 1: 2.   [d] 1 Cor. 16: 19. [f] 1 Thess. 2: 14.

use of the term, employed a few times in the New Testament to denote a popular assembly, in no way concerns this discussion. The generic use of the term, which, by a rhetorical figure, speaks, in a very few instances, of many churches in the singular number — just as we might speak generically of "the family in Russia" or "the college in France" without implying a confederation of Russian families or of French colleges — gives no new sense to the term, but only a special application of its second and ordinary sense.

Previous to the apostleship and conversion of Paul, as we learn from Acts, the principle that each church should elect its own officers had already been established by the eleven apostles at Jerusalem, when they instructed the church to choose for itself a subordinate class of officers, for the work of the diaconate; but the letters of Paul very forcibly enjoin the local church to exercise deference and kindly affection toward its officers, and, in connection with the deacons, to provide, for their pastors, adequate temporal support. From the Pauline letters, it is also evident that each true local church of Christ has, under the law of Christ, the right and duty of complete and exclusive self-government, by virtue of which, the whole body is to exclude unworthy members and, by necessary presupposition, to receive worthy ones;[a] to maintain careful discipline over its members, suppressing all disturbances and divisions; to manage its own pecuniary affairs; and, without imperilling their individual independence, or ignoring their individual responsibility to Christ, the churches have liberty to combine their means and influence to

[a] Cf. Acts 10: 47.

institute and conduct special Christian enterprises. [a]

With thorough, candid, inspection of the letters of Paul, and careful comparison of them with the rest of the New Testament, especially with the Acts, there need be no great difficulty, while this end is steadily kept in view, in ascertaining the nature of a New Testament church. Such a study of the subject can scarcely fail to make it evident that the great mass of nominal Christendom has, one way or another, departed very far from the simplicity of the New Testament and its well-defined, and by no means elaborate church model.

To call an ecumenical, national, or provincial organization of churches — whether allied or unallied to the state, whether governed by state officials, or by ecclesiastical prelates, or by both combined, or by other ecclesiastical

[a] Acts 11: 29, 30. Gal. 2: 10. 2 Cor. chapters 8 and 9.

representatives — to call such an organization, exercising dominion over the individual churches of which it is composed, a church, is to ignore and contravene the plain church principles of the New Testament.

In the light of the Pauline letters, many of our Baptist churches, in certain portions of the United States are not free from error and inconsistency in church polity. There is prevalent in the Baptist churches of New England and in those of many Northern and Western States, a system of things in relation to one feature of church polity, which is out of character with Baptist principles, and foreign to the New Testament.

The Baptist churches in question are, indeed, local, spiritual bodies of baptized believers, exercising their own internal discipline. But they have, for the most part, surrendered the control of the church property and revenues, and, therefore, much influence pertaining to the church, into the hands of mixed societies — societies composed of the adult members of the church and the adult members of the congregation, though the latter are, with rare exceptions, unconverted persons. In some instances, these societies, uniting the church and the world, are permitted to have a voice in the selection of pastors. These mongrel societies, and not the churches proper, are incorporated and recognized by the laws of the land. Not a few excellent brethren in these churches have acknowledged and deplored the evil of this state of things, and, in a measure, have sought to counteract it.

How this state of things came about by Baptists weakly conforming to their denominational and political environments, would be an instructive and admonitory story. How and when this now strongly entrenched and mischievous anomaly is to be rooted out, there is no prophet to foretell. The moral of it all is, Let Baptists, and all other Christians, beware how they connive at even the slightest aberration from the principles of the New Testament.

SECTION II.—THE OFFICERS OF THE CHURCH.

The writings of Paul fully describe the offices pertaining to a New Testament church.

The office of apostle was not filled by the selection, nor did it belong to the economy, of any one particular church or any combination of churches; but it was filled exclusively by the direct appointment of Christ, for the purpose of witnessing to Christ's resurrection, and of revealing and executing Christ's will in relation to all Christian things. From the nature of the case, as we have already seen, there were, and there could be, no successors to the original appointees.

The office of evangelist was that of preachers of the gospel, doing special missionary work of various sorts, without pastoral charge — and such, virtually, are many of our home and foreign missionaries in modern times; — but while the office, unlike that of the apostles, needed to be perpetuated for the wider dissemination of the gospel, and for special work of one kind and another in various individual churches, it belonged, like that of the apostles, to the internal economy of no particular church.

According to the Pauline Epistles, the offices pertaining to the economy of a New Testament church are two, and two only, in number — first, the office of bishop, presbyter, or pastor, as it is variously styled; and, secondly, the office of deacon; and in these

Epistles alone, have we a full account of both.

Paul uses the terms "bishop," or overseer, and "presbyter," or elder, interchangeably and as equivalent, as also does Peter; and they both connect the duties of a shepherd, or pastor, with the office designated by these terms.[a] The scholarly Episcopalians, Conybeare and Howson, candidly admit that "the terms 'bishop' and 'elder' are used in the New Testament as equivalent—the former denoting (as its meaning of overseer implies) the duties, the latter, the rank of the office." So, also, the learned Dean Alford, referring to Paul's interchangeable use of the terms "elder" and "bishop," speaks of "the fact of elders and bishops having been originally and apostolically synonymous."

The failure to recognize and prove loyal to this plain New Testament

[a] Acts 20: 28. 1 Pet. 1: 2.

teaching, is responsible for all the monstrous assumptions and pernicious innovations of the Romish and other hierarchies.

The duties of the pastoral office, with the qualifications for it, are clearly and fully set forth in Paul's letters to Timothy and Titus, in his address to the Ephesian elders,[a] and in a less direct, but equally convincing way, in his letters to the churches. In general terms, the duties of the pastoral office may be said to be to preach the gospel, to unfold the whole word of God, to interpret and administer the ordinances, to build up the Christian character of those under their care, to superintend the discipline of the church, to promote Christian activity and enterprise in the extension of the kingdom of Christ, and in the practice of Christian benevolence and mercy.*

[a] Acts 20: 17-35.

* See Appendix II. on Divine Estimate of the Pastoral Office.

In its primary sense, the Greek word διάκονος, translated "deacon," means simply a servant, often a waiting-man, and it is frequently used in the New Testament in the ordinary sense of servant, whether the service involved be lowly or lofty.

In its special and technical sense, as designating the second order of church officers, it is used but a few times in the New Testament, and, in these instances, chiefly by Paul. From the primary meaning of the term, from the way in which it is used when denoting the office of deacon, from the qualifications prescribed for the office, and from the duties assigned to it, serviceableness, thoroughgoing helpfulness, is the prime characteristic, the supreme purpose of the deaconship.

If we take the election and appointment of the "seven," to manage and assist in the distribution to the poor, recorded in Acts 6 : 1–7, as virtually the origination of the office, it becomes evident that deacons were designed to be helpers of the ministers of the word, by laboring specially in the temporal affairs of the church; and the qualifications for the office prescribed in Acts, and especially those in Paul's First Letter to Timothy,[b] show that they were to be helpers of the ministers of the word, by laboring to promote the harmony[c] of the church, to elevate its spiritual tone, and to advance its spiritual well-being and efficiency. The work of the deacons is not to govern, but to help the pastor, by serving tables,[d]—by providing, as it is often aptly expressed, for the table of the poor, for the table of the minister, and for the table of the Lord.

The office of deacon is no sinecure, no idle compliment, no empty honor; but an office designed for sagacious

[a] Acts 6: 3.
[b] 1 Tim. 3: 8-13.
[c] Acts 6: 1-3.
[d] Acts 6: 2, 3.

and loyal helpfulness, for self-sacrificing and plodding toil; an office eminently requiring for its right and full discharge, faith, humility, integrity, loyalty, wisdom, discreetness, sympathy, patience, liberality, consecration, and love.

The deaconship is a "business;"[a] and that business is the working up, developing, and caring for the finances of the church — for current expenses including pastoral support, for the relief of the poor, and for missionary enterprises at home and abroad. Because this truth is but little appreciated, and but slightly put into practice, the cause of Christ is languishing, in countless instances, the wide world over, in the midst of innumerable golden opportunities.

It would be an immense advantage to the cause of Christ, were suitable facilities for the proper training of

[a] Acts 6: 3.

deacons for their exceedingly important work, commonly available—were there a well-prepared and widely scattered literature of the subject, and a thorough and widely prevalent system of institute work for this purpose. Then, other things being equal, those most important enterprises on earth, home and foreign missions, with their educational implications, would not be hampered, imperilled, and all but paralyzed, for lack of "the sinews of war."

As it is, the culpable lack, or humiliating caricature, of Christian beneficence, and the careless or covetous withholding of untold millions of the Lord's money from the Lord's work, that are prevalent throughout Christendom, and that make its theory and practice so much at variance, in this particular, are attributable, in no small degree, to the common inappreciation, misconception, misuse, and neglect of the office of the diaconate; for all of which, not the deacons alone, but also the church and the ministry are, on many accounts, responsible.

One of the greatest perils of the divine institution of the diaconate is the modern, man-made invention of the trustee board, as it exists wherever prevail the previously mentioned mixed societies, constituted by the unequal yoking together of members of a Baptist church and unconverted people of its congregation, for the management of the church's pecuniary affairs. In these cases, which are very numerous, the trustee board, though a class of officials unknown to the New Testament, often becomes virtually an oligarchy, ruling the church and the pastor in many things, and usurping the principal functions of the diaconate, thereby reducing it to little more than a more or less ornamental nullity.

Besides this, in the many thousands of cases referred to, the trustee board is chosen, not by the church, but by the unhallowed amalgamation of the church and the world already spoken of; and as a consequence — except where churches with their anomalous societies, organize or reorganize as corporate bodies, under the provisions of recent state legislation — very frequently persons not connected with the church, and not converted, are chosen as members of the trustee board, and thus gain power to control the use of church property and to influence the policy of the church, in many important particulars.

Herein is manifest the evil and the insidiousness of the practice of substituting human devices for divine institutions. Deviation from Pauline or other apostolic principles, precedents, and precepts, blameworthy in any case, is specially inconsistent in churches pre-eminently professing to copy and uphold exclusively New Testament models.

When the real character and divinely assigned functions of the New Testament, and in particular, the writings of Paul, with their manifold and decisive bearings, are duly considered, it is evident that all ecclesiastical legislation on doctrines, ethics, institutions, and ordinances of Christianity is a presumptuous meddling with the ark of God, and an utter usurpation of the office of Christ and his apostles, who alone have legislative power in the church, and who, in the inspired Writings have given full revelation and spoken the last word on these subjects.

The attempts ecclesiastically to legislate all manner of Christians into nominal and superficial unity, by means of compromise and external organization, though attractive to the unthinking and unsettled, is a vain and ill-starred enterprise. There can be no true Christian unity except on the basis of the New Testament; and universal and complete return to the New Testament is the only way to bring it about. "Back to the New Testament" is the word.

SECTION III.—THE POSITION OF WOMAN IN THE CHURCH.

The writings of Paul determine definitely the position of woman in a New Testament church.

As to the divine bestowment of sonship to God, with all the accompanying blessings of salvation; as to faith in Christ as the divinely appointed means of procuring all these benefits; and as to baptism as the divinely prescribed form for avowing that faith, there is, as we learn from Paul, no distinction as to race, class, or sex—

"there can be neither Jew nor Greek, there can be neither bond nor free, there can be no male and female."[a]

But Christianity has not abolished the distinction of sex, either physically or ethically. Though, besides granting her an equal share with man, in the great salvation, Christianity has wrought marvels of mercy for womankind, relieving her of many grievous burdens, bestowing upon her many inestimable privileges, elevating the plane of her existence, and opening up to her many suitable spheres of usefulness; yet it has never contravened or ignored, but has ever sanctioned and insisted upon, the primary law of her being, her supplemental, auxiliary, and subordinate, though dignified and honorable, relation to man. Though Christ showed sympathetic interest in, and gracious respect for, womankind; though he drew women

[a] Gal. 3: 26–28.

in purest, warmest, and most reverential devotion to himself; though he imparted to them his most precious and sacred thoughts; though he constantly accepted their thoughtful and kindly ministrations; and though, at times, he employed them in important practical errands; yet it is the significant fact that he never called any woman to be an apostle, or to be a public preacher of the word. Though the apostles recognized and highly esteemed the glowing saintliness, the heroic loyalty, and the self-sacrificing devotion, characteristic of the best Christian women, yet these divinely inspired vicegerents of Christ never appointed women to fill either of the two constitutional offices of a Christian church; but directed that, in all cases, these offices should be filled by men.[a] Though Christianity has large use for the varied and facile powers of

[a] 1 Tim. 3: 1, 2. 2 Tim. 2: 2. Acts 6: 3. 1 Tim. 3: 12.

woman, and of the direct and indirect influence of woman, in the home, in society, and in the church, yet it ever avoids giving to her undue, or unnatural, publicity.

The writings of Paul strongly forbid women to speak, or to lead in prayer, in mixed public assemblies. "Let the women keep silence in the churches: for it is not permitted unto them to speak; but let them be in subjection, as also saith the law. And if they would learn anything, let them ask their own husbands at home: for it is shameful for a woman to speak in the church. What? was it from you that the word of God went forth? or came it unto you alone?"[a]

"If any man thinketh himself to be a prophet, or spiritual, let him take knowledge of the things which I write unto you, that they are the commandment of the Lord."[b] "I desire, there-

[a] 1 Cor. 14: 34–36.   [b] 1 Cor. 14: 37.

fore, that the men pray in every place, lifting up holy hands, without wrath and disputing. . . . Let a woman learn in quietness with all subjection. But I permit not a woman to teach, nor to have dominion over a man, but to be in quietness. For Adam was first formed, then Eve; and Adam was not beguiled, but the woman being beguiled hath fallen into transgression." [a]

Nothing could be more explicit than these apostolic injunctions.

The ripest exegetical scholars in all the world have with singular unanimity maintained that these passages positively forbid women to speak in mixed public assemblies. Here are a few specimens of their expositions of these, or of one or the other of these passages:

Dr. John A. Broadus: "Now it does not need to be urged that these

[a] 1 Tim. 2: 8, 11-14.

two passages from the Apostle Paul do definitely and strongly forbid that women shall speak in mixed public assemblies. No one can afford to question that such is the most obvious meaning of the apostle's commands."

Dr. A. C. Kendrick: "Both these usages—women's speaking in public assemblies, and sitting at meat in an idol's temple—he has mentioned twice in this epistle, and each time for a distinct purpose of censure."

Ellicott: "Every form of public address or teaching is clearly forbidden as at variance with woman's proper duties and destination."

Meyer: "After the apostle has forbidden to the woman any activity in the church assemblies as unbecoming to her, he now points to the destiny assigned her by God, the fulfilling of which brings salvation to her."

Neander: "Spiritual receptivity, and activity in domestic life, were recognized as the appropriate destiny of women; and therefore the female sex was excluded from the public discussion of religious subjects."

Godet: The apostle "draws the conclusion that the speaking of woman in public is in contradiction to the position assigned to her by the divine will expressed in the law."

Conybeare and Howson: "The apostle's meaning is that women are to be kept in the path of duty, not by taking upon themselves the office of the man (by taking a public part in the assemblies of the church, etc.), but by the performance of the peculiar functions which God has assigned her sex."

With these interpretations coincide those of Calvin, Lange, Hodge, Van Oosterzee, Stanley, Schaff, Alford, and many others.

As a general thing, through all the ages, the good taste, native modesty, and intuitive sense of Christian women, wherever unbeguiled by misguided or designing men, have readily perceived the meaning, acknowledged the propriety, and yielded to the authority of these divinely inspired apostolic commands.

Various, however, have been the attempts from divers quarters, to break or evade the force of this apostolic interdiction.

Sometimes it has been objected to the obvious meaning of 1 Cor. 14: 34–37, that inasmuch as Paul had mentioned the subject of women's speaking in public, in 1 Cor. 11: 5, without then and there condemning anything about it, but the unseemly manner of it, he can scarcely mean all that he seems to mean in the later passage. But in the former passage, Paul is condemning indecorous demeanor in public worship, and in the latter passage, he is censuring the maladministration of spiritual gifts; and the censure of the manner naturally belonged to the earlier topic, and the censure of the thing itself, to the later.

As Godet, Kendrick, and others point out, when considering this objection, Paul deals in the same way, in this same Epistle, with another subject of censure, the sitting at meat in an idol's temple. In 1 Corinthians 8: 9-13, he objects to the practice, as it might seem at first sight, only because it might give offense to weak brethren; but later on, in 1 Corinthians 10: 14-22, he condemns the thing in itself, as virtual idolatry.

There is no inconsistency in the apostle's method in either of these twofold censures; and the case must be desperate that depends upon setting the apostle at odds with himself.

Sometimes it has been objected, that the apostle must have intended that this prohibitory injunction should apply to the Corinthian church only.

But there is absolutely no evidence of this. On the contrary, Paul's first letter to "the church of God which is at Corinth"—the address of the letter thus implying that there was but one church in Corinth—says, "Let the women keep silence in the churches," thus making the prohibition applicable to all other churches. Besides this, the similar prohibition in Paul's First Letter to Timothy, a representative young minister, must have applied not only to the church in Ephesus, to which he then ministered, but also to all the churches to which, at any time, Timothy or any one else, might minister, as pastor or evangelist. There is a strong conviction upon the part of many eminent commentators, and the American Committee of Revision, that the prohibitory passage in First Corinthians should have attached to it the preceding clause, so as to read, "As in all the churches of the saints, let the women keep silence in the churches." Be that as it may, these prohibitory passages in First Corinthians and First Timothy, respectively, are, whether taken singly or together, unlimited as to place.

It has also sometimes been objected that the apostolic injunction under consideration could be of only temporary force, and must have long since become in fact, and according to original intention, a dead letter. But there is not the slightest hint in the Corinthian passage, or its context, that the command is anything less than perpetual in obligation. Besides the kindred interdiction in First Timothy is apostolically founded on two grounds that are as perpetual and as wide as humanity — the priority of man's creation and the priority of woman's transgression — "For Adam was first formed, then Eve; and Adam was not beguiled, but the woman being beguiled hath fallen into transgression."[a] The priority of Adam's creation indicated his natural headship; and Eve's priority of transgression indicated her greater liability to beguilement, and her natural unfitness for headship; and therefore the religious duties of speaking and praying in public assemblies were apostolically, and therefore, divinely, imposed exclusively on men. But whatever may be the precise logical sequence of the apostle's thought, it is unquestionable that he makes this injunction universal and perpetual, by basing it on grounds that are as lasting and as wide as the world. Remembering the dread curse[b] pronounced upon all those who add to, take from, or substitute anything for, any part of the word of God, who should dare to extirpate or tamper with this or any other portion of it?

[a] 1 Tim. 2: 13, 14.
[b] Gal. 1: 8, 9.   2 Peter 3: 15, 16.   Rev. 22: 18, 19.

Sometimes also, it has been thoughtlessly or venturesomely, objected that the Greek word λαλέω, a form of which is rendered "speak" in 1 Cor. 14: 34, 35, means "to babble;" and that, therefore, in that passage, women are only forbidden to babble in the churches — the apostle simply declaring that it is not permitted to women to babble, and that it is a shame for a woman to babble in a church. According to this extraordinary interpretation, does the passage imply that men never babble? or that they are fully permitted to babble? or that it is not disgraceful for women to babble, unless it is in a church? Is not babbling wrong and disgraceful in either men or women, at any time or anywhere?

While it is admitted that in classic Greek, some such signification of the word may sometimes be found, the ripest scholars, among them the late

Dr. John A. Broadus, find no instance of it in the New Testament. Various forms of the word are found many scores of times in its sacred pages, but never once do our translators give it the meaning of "babble," or anything like it. To "speak" is its true signification; and so it is commonly used in the New Testament, when God the Father, Christ, the Holy Spirit, angels, Moses, the prophets, the apostles, as well as others, are said to speak. There could be no more preposterous or presumptuous "babbling" than this attempt to substitute the word "babble" for the apostle's word "speak."

There are those who would arbitrarily restrict this apostolic interdiction to women speaking in the pulpit or on the platform. A person holding this view commonly says, in relation to this matter, "I draw the line at the pulpit and platform; but I would have women speak, without any restriction, on the floor of the house." But what the apostle says is not, " It is a shame for a woman to speak in a pulpit or on a platform; but " It is a shame"—a disgraceful thing — "for a woman to speak in the church"—in a mixed public assembly.

If woman were apostolically permitted to address mixed public assemblies, then, being shorter in stature and weaker in voice than men, she would have more need than men have of the elevation of the platform; and then if she were to retain any trace of the modesty that is the glory of her nature, the secret of her charm and power, she would sorely need whatever shelter the pulpit could afford her.

There are many who oppose the Pauline prohibition before us, with the argument from experience. It is said, the speaking of women in mixed public assemblies cannot be wrong, inasmuch as good has certainly come out of it. But useful as true experience, when far extended, correctly observed, and rightly interpreted, may be, in many of the affairs of life, it is wild, dangerous, impious, for any man or body of men, to set fallible notions of shallow human experience in direct opposition to express injunctions of the word of God. The interpretation of experience that runs counter to the divine word cannot be true, and if trusted and followed, it must, in the long run, bring on the evils against which the divine counsels and prohibitions were designed to guard. The highest wisdom of man is only folly, when it exalts itself above the wisdom and will of God.

It is easy to mistake the meaning of experience. A man may, for a time, preach the gospel effectually to others, and yet himself be not approved of God, and in the end become a castaway. Infidels have been converted to Christ, through their own mocking observance of the Lord's Supper and their own derisive mimicry of the preaching of the gospel, in their club-meeting revelry. Many converts to Christ have been made through the preaching of the gospel by men who ultimately proved themselves to be unconverted and corrupt at heart. Does it follow that infidels and other unconverted men are justified in preaching the gospel, derisively or otherwise, or that we would be justified in employing them thus to proclaim the gospel, or observe its ordinances? That God may bring some good out of the gospel truth spoken by Christian women, even when it is done in a way that is inconsistent with his express orders, is neither to be doubted, nor wondered at. But it is monstrous and perverse to say that

Christian women are, therefore, right, when they ignore and disobey certain injunctions and prohibitions of the divine word. However expedient and plausible it may seem to disregard and violate the word of God, at any point, it cannot fail to displease the Almighty, who says, "To obey is better than sacrifice, and to hearken than the fat of rams;"[a] and despite all apparent temporary advantages, it must, sooner or later, result in profound and far-reaching disaster. Through all the ages, the great and fatal departures from true and pure Christianity, in doctrine, polity, and practice, were brought about by men who considered themselves wiser than men who were divinely inspired, and who substituted their own vaporings about experience and expediency, for the word of God. "There is a way that

[a] 1 Sam. 15: 22.

seemeth right unto a man, but the end thereof are the ways of death." [a]

There are, in our day, a widespread disregard of, and hostility toward, the Pauline prohibition of women speaking in mixed public assemblies. Unfortunately, with many persons, the mere fact that the movement has an air of popular novelty is sufficient to establish, in their minds, its correctness and expediency, the Sacred Writings to the contrary notwithstanding. To such persons, the mere statement, "It has come to stay," appears cogent and unanswerable argument, in favor of any innovation, no matter how unscriptural it may be. But let it be remembered that Satan has come to stay; that infidelity, idolatry, and immorality have come to stay; and that nevertheless, the battle must be pressed to the gate against them uncompromisingly and persistently.

[a] Prov. 14: 12.

Any other course would be cowardice and treachery. Let the word of God, and not popular crazes and captivating innovations, be the supreme rule and standard on this and every other religious question. "Yea, let God be found true, but every man a liar."[a]

The tendency of the anti-Pauline woman's movement, so persistent in our day, is to subvert the three divine institutions — the family, the nation and the church; to unyoke the divine word from the neck of the conscience, and to dethrone God in human society. The movement tends to weaken the bonds of marriage, as its history and the present condition of things abundantly prove; and it renders the confusion of unscriptural divorces worse confounded. It seeks to introduce a new, subtle, and corrupting element into politics, already too corrupt, by foisting upon the nation

[a] Rom. 3: 4.

the principle of woman's suffrage. Apt indeed was Horace Bushnell's characterization of this feature of the movement, when he made the title of his book against it, "The Reform Against Nature." The good sense of the great majority of Christian women has endorsed his account of it, by persistently refusing to sanction the movement, and, as is well known, leading philosophic minds, of the sterner sex, Christian and non-Christian alike, that had once given a more or less tentative approval of the scheme, are now recoiling from it, and uttering notes of warning against it.

The leaders of the movement, as a rule, do not hesitate to proclaim war against the Sacred Writings — Old Testament and New Testament, Moses and Paul alike — wherever they do not coincide with their self-willed and revolutionary notions.

A lady, long prominent in a particular wing of a certain moral reform movement, but conspicuous, also, in the cause of woman's suffrage, with which she and others have sought to ally it, has said, when speaking of the Pauline prohibition of women speaking in mixed public assemblies, "Christ, not Paul, is my teacher." Yet she, like everyone else, could not know one syllable of Christ's teachings, except as Paul, or other apostles, or other inspired teachers, have reported them. We have precisely the same authority to prove Christ's declaration that, after his departure, his apostles would be divinely inspired, and that their words would not be their words, but his, as to prove that Christ uttered the Sermon on the Mount, or any other of his sayings whatsoever. To reject Paul, or Peter, or John, or any other apostle, is, therefore, to reject Christ. Their injunctions are the commandments of the Lord.

Another lady, very prominent in the woman's suffrage movement, most profanely says, "The women who crowd our Christian temples are sedulously taught their inferiority in the scale of being and their subjection to man as sovereign; and the Old Testament represents her as a marplot in creation, an afterthought, the orgin of sin in collusion with the devil, cursed of God in her maternity, and marriage made for her a slavery." "It is woman's position in the church and the Holy books accepted as authority, that make political equality so difficult." So, like many another leader and follower in the same and similar movements, she virtually says, "Away with the Bible, since, in the family, in the nation, and in the church, it places woman in a position auxiliary and in a measure subordinate to man!" Yet, even her sacrilegious utterances are less glaringly inconsistent than the course of those who, while professing to regard the Scriptures as the word of God, seek, nevertheless, to nullify its precepts, or evade their force, as if they were the puerile and fallacious inventions of man.

But these misguided utterances of the noted women just quoted, are but fair specimens of the sayings of the advance-guard of the movement in question, and are a true indication of its aims and spirit, and of its attitude toward Biblical Christianity.

It is very noticeable and significant, also, that this anti-Pauline, anti-Scriptural modern development, naturally aligns itself with, and finds its quickest growth among the votaries of disbelief and misbelief, among those who reject what is most distinctive and vital in Christianity and who embrace all manner of vagaries. Into what unnatural and perilous associations this movement would fain draw the true followers of Christ! It would be well if, with regard to this whole matter, Christian women, and Christian men, would "fear, lest by any means, as the Serpent beguiled Eve in his craftiness," their "minds should be corrupted from the simplicity and purity that is toward Christ."

But one of the most significant and astounding of isolated indications in connection with modern anti-Paulinism is the fact that a man of talents and attainments, high in the councils of a great Christian institution of learning, should venture to say, with reference to the matter in hand, "Men are not going to perpetuate a foolish custom, if an apostle himself advised it." To how giddy a height can human presumption ascend! That, too, in the face of the apostle's warning declaration in relation to the matter, "If any man thinketh himself to be a prophet, or spiritual, let him take knowledge of the things which I write unto you, that they are the commandment of the Lord"!

But let us turn for a moment to a different phase of the subject. The vast characteristic distinctions between the sexes, in the economy of human nature, are radical and ineradicable.

As his physical structure, mental composition, and dominant impulses preordain, it is characteristic of man, in nature, society and art, to originate, form, and achieve. With regard to woman, on the other hand, as her physical organism, constitutional aptitudes and proclivities render inevitable, it is characteristic of her in the economy of human nature, to supplement, aid, sympathize and cherish. It is hers to give sanctuary and nourishment to embryo and infant, to nurture and mould the child, to be the helper and solace of manhood, and the emollient and moral and emotional atmosphere of the home. In this sphere she finds her highest function, her natural adaptation, her truest happiness.

The natural relations of the sexes are the union of principal and auxiliary; the harmony of complemental differences.

In answer to those who say that the subordinate and auxiliary relation of woman toward man is the result of degeneracy of womanly type and the primal and perpetual domination of man, it is sufficient to say, that as all the vital forces of both sexes unite in the perpetuation of the race, there can be no degeneracy or improvement of type in any new generation, in which the sexes do not equally share; and that the persistently subordinate and auxiliary position of the female sex through all history cannot be accounted for otherwise than on the grounds of woman's natural tendency and instinctive choice.

Elevating and refining culture, so far from tending to abolish these distinctions, emphasizes them, and renders the types of male and female more divergent. It is only among the more degraded and savage tribes, where brutality is most prevalent and most unrelieved that the great distinctions between the sexes are least observable, and the woman is least differentiated from the man.

Manhood and womanhood, when at their highest development and best estate, manifest most of all, their organic yet harmonious differences of type.

In all this, the book of nature and the book of Scripture agree; and the Pauline precepts, given by divine inspiration, concerning the position of women in the church, accord with the voice of God, concerning her, in creation and nature.

Those, therefore, who, whether men or women, rebel against these Pauline prohibitions, fight against nature and against God.

There is this consolation, however, for those who, in these times of upheaval and confusion, tremble for the safety of the ark of God, for the permanence of Christian institutions, for the supremacy of Scripture, that inasmuch as nature and Scripture are in profound accord and cannot utterly be overthrown, no matter how great and pernicious the perversions and evils of any particular time may be, the true people of Christ must finally return to the absolute rule of the divine word; and the latest Christian centuries must conform to the principles divinely laid down for their guidance in the first.

To close the matter up, it is evident, in view of the clearly proved apostolic functions and authority of Paul, that his writings, which treat so fully of the matter, have a decisive practical bearing on the subject of church order in all its departments.

Chapter X.

PRACTICAL BEARING ON ESTIMATE OF CHRISTIAN ATTAINMENTS.

As they plainly claim and abundantly prove, the Holy Scriptures are divinely constituted the supreme standard of truth and right, and the final test of all opinions and practices, whether of long standing or of recent origin, whether generally prevailing or of only local acceptance. Till the end of time, all things are to be tried by the word. "To the law and to the testimony! if they speak not according to this word, surely there is no morning for them."[a] "They have Moses and the prophets; let them hear them."[b] "And as many as walk by this rule, peace be upon

[a] Isa. 8:20. [b] Luke 16:29.

them, and mercy, and upon the Israel of God."[a] "And we have the word of prophecy made more sure; whereunto ye do well that ye take heed, as unto a lamp shining in a dark place."[b] Such are the claims of the Scriptures to the place of supreme authority in all matters of faith and practice; and they are not to be disputed.

We have already seen that the writings of Paul, being divinely inspired and being a constituent part of the divinely prescribed standard of truth and right, are invested with the absolute authority characteristic of, and inseparable from, Holy Scripture.

Now, the Pauline writings distinctly claim to be the infallible touchstone, the final test, of all attainments in Christian things: "If any man thinketh himself to be a prophet, or spiritual, let him take knowledge of the things which I write unto you, that

[a] Gal. 6 : 16.   [b] 2 Pet. 1 : 19.

they are the commandment of the Lord."[a] This bold and crucial Pauline challenge — selected as the motto, and furnishing the motive of, this work — clearly teaches and firmly insists that no claims to spiritual and high religious light that do not accord with the writings of Paul are to be honored or recognized.

We are thus bound by the highest authority to accept and employ the writings of Paul as the decisive criterion of all pretensions to special spiritual insight and superior religious light.

In the third section of the immediately preceding chapter, the specious argument from experience, designed to justify departure from, or modification of, the rule of Scripture, was considered and confuted. It was shown that the genuineness of religious experience and the justness of its

[a] 1 Cor. 14:37.

interpretation must be tested by Scripture, and that Scripture is neither to be condemned nor disparaged on the shallow ground of so limited and misinterpretable a thing as mere human experience. It was shown, also, that if argument from experience does not coincide with the writings of Paul, or with any other portion of Scripture, the experience is spurious, or the interpretation of it is false. On this point, nothing further need be added for the purposes of this discussion.

At various periods in the history of Christianity, there have arisen influential persons or sects claiming possession of high religious light derived from other sources than the Scriptures, and supplementing, modifying, or superseding the Scriptures in whole or in part.

Early in the third century, the celebrated Origen, a theologian of stupendous intellect and intellectual industry, but saturated with the Platonic philosophy, seriously perverted and paganized much of the Christianity of his own and later times, by pouring his Platonism into his theology, and by indulging his propensity to interpret Scripture in an arbitrary, fanciful, and highly allegorical way — a way which has reproduced itself in many minds, in all succeeding ages. Against this self-willed, imaginative and sophistical tendency, how sharply the warning of Paul rings out: "Take heed lest there shall be any one that maketh spoil of you through his philosophy and vain deceit, after the tradition of men, after the rudiments of the world, and not after Christ"![a] It would have been well for the cause of truth, in all ages, if Origen and all others had given due heed to that Pauline admonition, and to this Paul-

[a] Col. 2 : 8.

ine injunction: "If any man thinketh himself to be a prophet, or spiritual, let him take knowledge of the things which I write unto you, that they are the commandment of the Lord."

In consequence of the great intellectual, political, and religious upheavals of the sixteenth century, when, after ages of mental and spiritual stagnation, the minds of men sprang into volcanic activity concerning the greatest of human interests, both temporal and spiritual, there developed, at different times thereafter, a strong tendency to mysticism, which, as the etymology of the term suggests, is a closing of the eyes to the ordinary and external source of religious light—that is, the Scriptures—and a looking for spiritual enlightenment from an inner and preternatural source, virtually a divine revelation to, and within, each individual.

Several sects, organically unconnected, holding these or similar views, claiming peculiar subjective light, chiefly on matters of statecraft, philosophy, morals, and religion, and bearing the arrogant title of *Illuminati*, arose in the sixteenth, seventeenth, and eighteenth centuries, in various parts of Europe and Asia. Most of them believed that by mental abstraction, uninterrupted passive contemplation, and mystic devotion to God, a divine light was shed upon the soul, through a supernatural sense, and in a transcendental way. These, instead of testing their inner light by the Scripture, tested the Scripture by their inner light; and thus naturally came to reject the Scripture, for the most part, or altogether—thereby setting an example that has been eagerly followed by many in the present day.

In 1648, George Fox, a young Englishman, unlettered, but much given to religious meditation and revery, having come to believe that in every human being in all the world, there is an inner light, furnished by Christ and by the Holy Spirit, sufficient, without the Scriptures, to secure the salvation of men, if that light were duly used, devoted himself to the work of preaching the doctrine of the universal inner light, as largely superseding all other lights, and to that of showing the necessity of trying men's opinions and religions by the Holy Spirit rather than by the Scriptures. His message was virtually a protest against what he regarded as the excessive "scripturalism" of that age. It was in reality, largely a protest against the dead formalism in religion, characteristic of the time; but, in his unguarded recoil from that, he landed into the mystical spiritualities and practical grotesqueries that have characterized so many of his followers ever since.

It must not be overlooked, however, that a large number of his followers, known as Quakers or the Society of Friends, have come in later times into much closer accord with the beliefs of evangelical Christians generally, as several of their published statements of belief clearly show — though, indeed, the denomination has been far from uniform in its tenets; yet, such is the force of the doctrine of the "inner light" still potent among them, though less distinctly avowed than in former times, that they reject altogether the Christian ordinances of baptism and the Lord's Supper, as too "unspiritual" for their etherealized notions of what is becoming to the gospel dispensation, and on the same principle, they reject also the scriptural rule that women shall not be public preachers of the gospel.

The opinion that the Holy Spirit in the mind of the individual believer, at any time contravenes and cancels his own inspired word — and it has gained much currency in our day — is a nourisher of carnal self-sufficiency and spiritual pride, and is a common source of delusions and snares. "To the law and to the testimony! if they speak not according to this word, surely there is no morning for them."[a]

"If any man thinketh himself to be a prophet, or spiritual, let him take knowledge of the things which I write unto you, that they are the commandment of the Lord."

One of the most remarkable and erratic of all the mystics was Emmanuel Swedenborg — born 1688, died 1772. Till his fifty-fifth year his life was given to business, science, and philosophy; but for nearly thirty years, the latter part of his life was devoted to theology and spiritualism. His native strength of intellect, his scientific and

[a] Isa. 8: 20.

philosophic attainments, his exuberant imagination and fancy render his religious lucubrations of a highly intellectual order, yet as full of vagaries and phantasmagoria as an opium-eater's dream.

Taking the subtle and fantastic products of his prolific and overheated brain as genuine revelations from God, though unsubstantiated by either miracle or fulfilled prophecy, he refused to test them by the apostolic letters, but actually sought to test the Sacred Writings by them; and finding many parts of Scripture incapable of being warped so as to endorse his ideas and theories, he rejected thirty-two out of the sixty-six books of Scripture — of the New Testament he rejected all but the Gospels and the Apocalypse. In his alleged interviews with angels and spirits of men from heaven and hell — apostles, prophets, and others — they are made to lose their own individuality and to speak the dialect and the ideas of Swedenborg. As Emerson says, "All his interlocutors Swedenborgianize."

Had Swedenborg recognized and reverenced the divine inspiration and authority of Paul's writings, and tested his meditations by them, instead of testing them by his meditations, he would have saved himself and others from rejecting one-half of the entire word of God, and nearly all that is distinctive in Christianity, and would have saved the world from a deluge of morbid and perverse imaginings.

The transparent and impudent imposture of Mormonism, founded on pretended visions and revelations of the crudest and most bizarre description, could never stand any serious application of the test of Scripture to its doctrines, its institutions, or its morals. Though of vastly lower moral grade than Swedenborgianism,

Mormonism has nevertheless, several strains of kinship with it, particularly its spiritualism and its anthropomorphic conceptions of God. It shows distinctly to what low levels spurious Christians can sink, and into what far-off regions they can wander, when they cast themselves off from the moorings of Scripture and embark on the wild sea of their own vain imaginings and the world's alluring lies.

Modern Spiritualism, like ancient necromancy, is an attempt to procure light concerning the unseen and future world by means of communications, to the living, from spirits of the dead. The system is a revivification and combination of the necromantic superstitions of remote ages and widely separated peoples. Swedenborgianism has had much to do, at least indirectly, with preparing for it, and with bringing it about. The latter half of the nineteenth century, a decidedly materialistic period, has witnessed the rapid development of this ghostly superstition. Despite the poverty and inconsequentiality of its revelations, the imbecile gibberish of its alleged communications from the mighty departed, the frequent and thorough exposure of its fraudulent phenomena, and the evident perniciousness of its fruits, Spiritualism has proved fascinating to people of a certain marvel-mongering and fanatical type and tendency, in positions high and low. Notoriously, it is a peril both to right reason and to Christian faith. Devout reverence for, and implicit deference to, the writings of Paul and the word of God generally, are the specific antidote and prophylactic for this moonstruck superstition and anti-Christian craze.

Originating in the latter third of the nineteenth century, and assuming the pretentious name of "Christian

Science," though innocent both of Christian doctrine and the scientific method, one of the most crass and pernicious of popular delusions is now running its course. It claims to be a new discovery of vital truth and mental power, by which the Bible is to receive unique and authoritative interpretation, and the world, relief from all manner of evils, mental and physical alike. It may well be said of this new discovery of truth, that what is true in it is not new, and what is new in it is not true; and furthermore, that the great mass of it is only a farrago of old or revamped philosophical crudities and absurdities. It bases itself on the sophistical doctrines of monism and extreme idealism, which teach that matter and all its phenomena, even such as body disease, are unreal; that there is only one substance; that the one substance is spirit; that spirit is God; and that God is all.

Thus its logical trend is toward some species of pantheism.

It denies personality to God, alleging that personality involves finiteness; and, therefore, it makes the personality of Jesus merely human, though in view of a divine indwelling in him, it is pleased politely and poetically to call him "divine." Denying the reality of matter, and, therefore, the reality of disease, it instructs its votaries to regard all physical evil as non-existent, as a mere figment of the imagination. Regarding the reality of physical evil and moral evil, alike, as inconsistent with the goodness of God, and both, therefore, unreal, it proposes to train its adherents to doubt and scout all physical and moral evil out of the world. This preposterous unbelief of obvious verities, it ventures to call *faith*—instead of credulity and presumption.

That vigorous and cheerful minds

may often beneficially influence persons subject to various nervous disorders and morbid mental states is known to nearly every one; but to dignify this truism with the title of "mind healing," flourishing it before all the world as a great discovery, and offering it as a panacea for all the ills that flesh is heir to, is arrant charlatanism.

Like the Hagelian philosophy, which minimizes the function of conscience and the notion of sin, the "Christian Science" craze inevitably belittles the sinfulness of sin, renders nugatory the atonement of Christ and the regeneration of the Spirit, and repudiates the full inspiration and authority of Scripture. Founded upon sophistical lies in philosophy and upon daring negations of what is distinctive and fundamental in Christianity, it naturally develops delusion in thought, maudlinism in sentiment, and laxness in morals. Invented by a woman with whom marriage was a failure, it boldly seeks to subvert the relations of the sexes as divinely determined in creation and redemption.

Brought to the test of Paul's writings, or of the word of God as a whole, its folly and falsity become manifest, and it appears in its true character as "profane and vain babblings, and oppositions of science falsely so called."[a]

Right in line with the many forms of inner-light-ism strung along the ages, the so-called "Christian consciousness," conspicuous in these latter decades, has been asserting the vast claim of being either an independent, co-ordinate, or collateral source of religious light.

As the metaphysicians and lexicographers, in general, maintain, agreeably to the derivation of the word,

[a] 1 Tim. 6: 20 A. V.

consciousness is a knowledge and an accompanying knowledge, a knowing of one's own self, of one's own existence and identity, in intimate connection with a knowing of one's own states and activities. It is a knowledge of one's own being, in union with a knowledge of one's own action or passion, to use the latter word in its older sense. Consciousness may be said to be the personal perception of self, together with the personally perceived self-registration of one's own thoughts, feelings, and activities.

In its own sphere, the authority of consciousness is absolute — from it there can be no appeal. Our sense of what we actually think, feel, or will, is developed in consciousness alone.

But it is not the function of consciousness to determine the objective truth of the thoughts present in the mind, the legitimacy of its feelings, or the wisdom of its volitions. All that belongs to the reasoning faculty, broadly considered; and the only business that consciousness has to do with these things is to record their simple presence in the mind, without pronouncing on their quality or their validity. Thus so far as the proper function of consciousness is concerned, its deliverances are just as valid in a heathen as in a Christian, in a lunatic as in a sane man. It simply records upon the tablets of the cognitive self, the impressions made upon the mind, whether these are the vagaries of the insane, or the normal mental action of the sane, whether they are the superstitious thoughts, feelings, and volitions of the heathen, or the well-founded, well-digested, well-defined experiences of the highest type of Christians. The ablest and safest metaphysicians, from Kant to Calderwood, so teach, substantially.

But many advocates of the new

theology, desiring, in some measure, to supplement, modify, or supersede the teachings of the Scripture, strive to attain their end by assigning to consciousness, or at least to the consciousness of Christians, or, as they call it, "Christian consciousness," an entirely new and impossible function —that of being an organ of objective knowledge. They would make it an authority on doctrine and ethics. Whatever in Scripture accords with their Christian consciousness, they accept; whatever in Scripture does not accord with their Christian consciousness, they reject; and whatever in Scripture has not as yet found or reached their Christian consciousness, they superciliously ignore. Many go even further, and claim that their Christian consciousness is a real and safe light and guide where the Scripture is silent. Thus they regard Christian consciousness as a sort of divine inspiration, differing, it may be, in degree, but not in kind, from that of prophets and apostles.

But if Christian consciousness were what is thus claimed for it — a divine illumination and quasi-inspiration — its utterances would be the same, or consistent, in all Christian souls. Yet it is notorious that there is no unity, but only diverseness and discord in the deliverances of the Christian consciousnesses of the many who profess faith in Christian consciousness as a source of objective knowledge. By thus assigning to consciousness a function entirely foreign to its nature and design, and belonging solely to the intellect, it comes to pass that consciousness, whose deliverances in its own proper sphere are final, is made responsible for the objective validity and divine revelation of the vagaries, caprices, and whims of each individual, and, logically, those of all individuals, however contradictory or absurd. This is to make human notions of the fitness of things, and human impressions and impulses of all sorts, the test of the Scriptures, the superior of the Word of God.

Now, neither "Christian" consciousness nor non-Christian consciousness is, or can be, a source of objective truth, either independently or subordinately. The consciousness of a true Christian has, indeed, or may have, a deep impression of his intellectual, moral, and spiritual perception and reception of Christian truth; and it may thus enable him more vividly to realize its preciousness and power. But we are all dependent solely upon the understanding for the perception of truth; and the understanding is dependent on the Scriptures for distinctively Christian truth, and upon the Holy Spirit's interpretive and strengthening influence for the fullest, clearest, and most effectual apprehension of the truth in Scripture.

If, as is really the case, a Christian's consciousness differs nothing from any other consciousness, either in kind, in function, or in validity; if, as is equally true, it differs from any other consciousness merely in its content; and if, as is no less true, it receives its content, like any other consciousness, only through the intellect, it would appear that the term "Christian," as applied to consciousness, is largely a misnomer, and that the joining of these two words is no more suitable as a discriminative, distinctive appellation, than would be such terms as "Christian intellect," "Christian faculties," "Christian anatomy," and "Christian physiology."

If the deliverances of "Christian consciousness" do not accord with the writings of Paul, or with any other part of the word of God, the true nature and office of consciousness have been misunderstood, and the errors of the head, of the heart, or of the consequently warped conscience, have been mistaken, as, with the "Christian consciousness" theory, they often are, for its utterances. "To the law and to the testimony! if they speak not according to this word, surely there is no morning for them."[a] "If any man thinketh himself to be a prophet, or spiritual, let him take knowledge of the things which I write unto you, that they are the commandment of the Lord."

Closely connected, at some points, with the "Christian consciousness" error, is a prevalent delusion of subtle, seductive, and very serious character, relative to a particular part of the work of the Holy Spirit upon believers. Like many another dangerous error, it is the perversion of an important and precious truth.

[a] Isa. 8: 20.

The work of the Holy Spirit in leading and helping the people of God — in their thinking, loving, choosing, and attempting; in their praying, praising, and preaching; and in the exercise of all the functions and activities of spiritual life — is something that, as followers of Christ, we are taught in Scripture to believe in, to seek for, to expect, to rely upon, and to be assured of. There can be no warrantable doubt that in all the forms of duty, active and passive alike, true believers are led and aided by the Spirit of God. "As many as are led by the Spirit of God, these are the sons of God."[a] "The Spirit also helpeth our infirmity: for we know not how to pray as we ought; but the Spirit himself maketh intercession for us with groanings which cannot be uttered; and he that searcheth the hearts knoweth the mind of the Spirit, because he

[a] Rom. 8: 14.

maketh intercession for the saints according to the will of God."[a] Unspeakably great and precious are the privileges of believers in the leading and help of the Spirit.

Notwithstanding the certainty of these things, it is a gross delusion and a perilous snare to believe, as many unguarded souls are coming to believe, that the Spirit of God makes to believers distinct revelations of divine truth and of the divine will, other than, and independent of, what he has already set forth in his Holy Word. That he inclines and enables human souls to understand, receive, love, and obey the inspired word is certain; and that, in a secret yet effectual way, he leads the people of God in the way of life is not to be doubted. But, like many of the most vital processes in animated nature, these things are done below consciousness. It is not possi-

[a] Rom. 8: 26, 27.

ble to separate in consciousness between the work of the Spirit of God and our own spiritual activities. Profession of ability to make such a distinction in consciousness is the unfailing sign of fanaticism and the very earmark of delusion. The results of the Spirit's work, such as faith, repentance, love, reverence, obedience, prayerfulness, joy, and peace, come into consciousness of course—these being personal states or activities of the soul—but the Spirit's direct action upon the soul is entirely secret and hidden.

It is a prominent characteristic of the presumptuous delusion now under consideration, that its victims often come to regard their own arbitrary and capricious notions, their morbid impulses and disordered fancies, as direct communications from the Spirit of God.

A medical expert has alleged that

the phenomena of snakes present in optical illusion, to the victim of delirium tremens is caused by the congestion of a network of extremely minute veins in a thin transparent membrane of the eye, and the consequent projecting of the increased and serpentine venous circulation upon the field of vision. Thus the delirious inebriate sees simply the minute and tortuous circulation of the vital fluid in his disordered eye; but he imagines that he sees serpents of the largest size and most horrible and deadly description. Even so, by projecting their own presumptuous thoughts, ambitious aspirations, and arbitrary inclinations, upon the field of their mental vision, the votaries of this subtle craze mistake the subjective for the objective, and mistake their own minds for the mind of God. But fanatical presumption needs to be guarded against, quite as much as rationalistic doubt.

When they are wishing to evade the force of certain Scripture commands or prohibitions that are distasteful to them, there are those who delude themselves into the belief that they receive from the Spirit of God, inward answers to their prayers, relieving them from the obligations imposed upon them by Scripture. This is a monstrous self-deception, a blasphemous presumption. It is not, and it could not be, the way of "the Spirit of truth" to produce in the minds of his people repudiations, or modifications, of the divine word which he himself inspired—he cannot deny himself.

This, like all other pretensions to superior religious light, other than that derivable from the Scriptures, must be brought to the crucial and decisive test of Scripture: "To the law and to the testimony! if they speak not according to this word, surely there is no morning for them." "If any man thinketh himself to be a prophet, or spiritual, let him take knowledge of the things which I write unto you, that they are the commandment of the Lord."

The brilliant advance in educational methods, in physical science, in mechanical inventions, in travelling facilities, and in material comforts, during the last few decades, seems to have turned the heads, hardened the hearts, and perverted the moral judgments of many of the men of our time to such an extent that they neither perceive the spiritual glory of the Scripture, nor realize their need of its illuminating power. Thus the light that is in them is darkness; and "how great is that darkness"!

Apart from the beneficent influence of Scripture, the present age is morally as blind, corrupt, and helpless as any of its predecessors; and even now, wherever the Sacred Writings are widely discarded, a strong tendency to revert to the barbarisms and vice of the darkest ages is distinctly manifest.

All modern claims and pretensions to superior religious attainments, must, like those of every earlier, and every later, century, be tested by the supernatural light that streams down to us from the first century, through the atmosphere of the Sacred Writings; and by these Writings, the Writings of Paul included, must the principles and practices, with the claims and pretensions, of this, and of all the centuries, be finally judged.

Neither attainments in physical science, burrowings among the roots of dead or living languages, saturations of pagan and paganizing philosophies, nor achievements in any other pursuit whatsoever, can ever qualify or warrant any man to sit in judgment upon the divine word. The most distinguished preacher, the most noted theological professor, or the most influential religious journalist, must be condemned, who, in the smallest particular, ventures to override, or fails humbly to sit at the feet of, inspired apostles, whose words, the Saviour said, would be, not their words, but his words, and the words of the Spirit who inspired them. Hostile criticisms upon divinely inspired writings are the vaporings of presumptuous folly and rebellious self-conceit.

Whatever in our civilization and customs, whatever in our religious views and ways, whatever in our church practices and pursuits, whatever in our women's movements and organizations, and whatever in our societies and methods for the religious training and culture of the young, are inconsistent with apostolic precept or precedent, must, on pain of divine displeasure, and of disastrous consequences sooner or later, be conformed to the divine standard of the Sacred Writings in general, and, in particular, the Writings of Paul.

"IF ANY MAN THINKETH HIMSELF TO BE A PROPHET, OR SPIRITUAL, LET HIM TAKE KNOWLEDGE OF THE THINGS WHICH I WRITE UNTO YOU, THAT THEY ARE THE COMMANDMENT OF THE LORD."

APPENDIX.

I.

THE FIVE-LINKED CHAIN.*

A STUDY OF A GROUP OF PAULINE DOCTRINES IN ROMANS 8: 29, 30.

"For whom he foreknew, he also foreordained to be conformed to the image of his Son, that he might be the first-born among many brethren: and whom he foreordained, them he also called: and whom he called, them he also justified: and whom he justified, them he also glorified."

The Epistle to the Romans is the heart of the Pauline Writings, and, indeed, of the whole New Testament; and the brief passage before us is the heart of the Epistle to the Romans. This microcosm of Holy Writ deserves our most earnest and devout attention.

In demonstrating the completeness and security of those who are in Christ, the apostle has adduced, in the previous part of the Epistle, the vicarious and redemptive work of Christ in

* This dissertation, from the pen of the author of this book, was published, April, 1886, in the *Baptist Quarterly Review*. Presenting a group of leading and characteristic Pauline doctrines, it is here reproduced as a pendant to Chapter VII., in the body of this work.

their behalf, the quickening and sanctifying operations of the Holy Spirit in their souls, and the benignant acts of God the Father toward them in justifying, adopting, preserving, and enriching them. It is further shown that, under the gracious control of God, nothing can effectually work against, and that in reality everything must work for, the interest of true believers. "We know," says the apostle, " that to them that love God all things work together for good, *even* to them that are called according to *his* purpose."[a] Thus true Christians are described, from the human side, as those who love God,—love to God being evidently regarded as the summary and essence of Christian character and duty; and they are described, from the Divine side, as those "who are called according to" God's "purpose,"— the being called according to his purpose being obviously considered as the root, or as the well-spring, of love to God and of similar gracious qualities in any human breast. At this point, the passage under consideration comes in, as further explanatory and descriptive of the call according to God's purpose: "For whom he foreknew, he also foreordained *to be* conformed to the image of his Son, that he might be the first-born among many brethren : and whom he foreordained, them he also called : and whom he called, them he also justified : and whom he justified, them he also glorified." The logic of the passage has, for its major premise,

[a] Rom. 8 ; 28.

God's eternal purpose of grace; for its minor premise, God's calling of certain human souls into the exercise of faith toward Christ, love toward God, and kindred Christian graces; and, for its conclusion, the final salvation and glory of all who are effectually called.

It is important to observe that the five verbs, προέγνω, προώρισεν, ἐκάλεσεν, ἐδικαίωσεν, ἐδόξασεν, translated, respectively, "foreknew," "foreordained," "called," "justified," "glorified," are in the aorist tense, the well-known function of which is to predicate completed action without special reference to time when. These verbs tell us what God did in purpose in the eternal past; for, from the nature of the case and from the plain intimation of Scripture, his purpose is, and must be, an eternal purpose. All that God does in fact, he does in accordance with his eternal purpose; and all that God has done in purpose, he does in the fulness of time, in fact. Both with man and with God, the purpose is the moral essence of the act. With man, it is true, because of his blindness, weakness, and changeableness, to will and to do are seldom commensurate and identical; but with God, to purpose and to perform are, virtually and morally, ever one and the same. With God, the purpose and the result are inevitably linked together, and invariably and exactly coincide. God "foreknew," "foreordained," "called," "justified," "glorified," in eternal purpose, all those, and none other than those, whom, "in the coming on of time," he eventually calls, justifies, and glorifies in fact. The aorist is also singularly well-fitted, and, in the New Testament, is often used, to express the virtual completion of the divine act in the divine purpose; and Christ employed it very strikingly, when, in his own personal and official prayer, at the conclusion of his valedictory discourse, though the cross and the grave were still before him, he thus appealed to his eternal Father, in the inflexible purpose and in the unwavering confidence of his heart : "I glorified thee on the earth, having accomplished the work which thou hast given me to do." Thus, in virtually identifying the divine purpose and the divine act in the passage before us, the great apostle has closely followed the example of his Divine Lord.

In addressing ourselves more directly to the study of this five-linked chain of gospel truth and grace, let us first of all determine, substantially, and with as much exactness as possible, the sense in which the term προέγνω, or "foreknew," representing the *first link* in the chain, is here to be taken. To interpret this word as expressing mere naked prescience would give no adequate sense; for the good and the bad, the finally saved and the finally lost, are equally objects of divine foresight. The term "foreknew" is evidently here used to characterize and distinguish the attitude and action of the divine mind toward those, and those only, whom God has, from all eternity, designed to make his own peculiar people. Nor may we mentally supply, as some interpreters have attempted to do, some such words as "would repent, believe, love and obey"; for there is no evident ellipsis in the passage; nay, there is evidently no ellipsis in the passage. The sense is complete as it stands; and to supply such words, or their opposites, or any other words, is eisegesis and not exegesis, is interpolation and not interpretation. Such treatment sets the passage in direct opposition to the plainest teachings of the apostle, not only in this but in other Epistles, as witness the following specimen passages: God "saved us, and called us with a holy calling, not according to our works, but according to his own purpose and grace, which was given us in Christ Jesus before times eternal."[a] Again, "he chose us in him before the foundation of the world, that we should be holy and without blemish before him in love."[b] Once more, "By grace have ye been saved through faith; and that not of yourselves: *it is* the gift of God: not of works, that no man should glory. For we are his workmanship, created in Christ Jesus for good works, which God afore prepared that we should walk in them."[c]

The inserting of certain words after the word "foreknew," in the manner already indicated, has the effect of substituting the consequent for the antecedent, the end for the means, the effect for the cause. In that act of

[a] 2 Tim. 1:9.   [b] Eph. 1:4.   [c] Eph. 2:8–10.

gracious omnipotence, accomplished by the Spirit of God in the souls of those who are in process of being saved, and variously denominated in Scripture, a new creation, a new birth, and a resurrection, the soul, from the nature of the case, is and must be passive; though, indeed, in consequence of that quickening and renewing energy, it is sure to become active in the exercise of faith, love, obedience and other Christian virtues. To say, then, that God makes the foresight of such spiritual qualities in human souls as could come to be in them only as the effect of his own sovereign and regenerating grace, the motive and *raison d'etre* of his favorable regard, is to reason in a circle and to become involved in an absurdity. These two senses, therefore, for the word "foreknew"—the sense of naked prescience, and that of prescience of gracious qualities quite gratuitously attributed—must be rejected as unscriptural and absurd.

What, then, is the sense in which "foreknew" is here to be taken? It must be evident to every one capable of analyzing thought and of weighing the force of language, that to know or to foreknow a person is something different from, and more complex than, to perceive or to anticipate a fact. But in order clearly to determine the significance of the word as here used, it is of great advantage to consider somewhat carefully the Scripture usage with respect to the word "know." It is obvious that the word "know" is frequently employed in the Sacred Writings in quite another than the primary and literal sense, though it will be found that the derived and secondary meaning is a legitimate outgrowth, according to recognized philological laws, from the literal and primary. The usage of the New Testament, with respect to the word "know," closely resembles that of the Old Testament; in fact, there is a decidedly Hebraistic element in the New Testament use of the word; and the reasons are not far to seek. The religious conceptions of the writers of the New Testament were formed largely by their familiarity with the Old Testament Scriptures; and their evidently intimate acquaintance with the Septuagint, the Greek version of the Hebrew Scriptures commonly used in their day, naturally accustomed them to use several important words of the Greek language in a somewhat Hebraistic sense. Thus they came to use the Greek γινώσκω in the pregnant sense, and as the full equivalent, of the Hebrew *yada*. Both of these words are used in the Old and New Testaments respectively, to represent acts of the understanding, of the moral judgment, of the affections, and of the will. Both are used in the senses of love, choose, approve, appoint, and in the complex sense of recognize, claim, and acknowledge as one's own. Both are used to express God's favorable regard and gracious love, as in Amos, 3:2, "You only have I known of all the families of the earth," and in

1 Cor. 8:3, "If any man loveth God, the same is known of him." Both are used to convey the idea of divine approval, as in Ps. 1:6, "The Lord knoweth the way of the righteous," and in Matt. 7:23, and 25:12, "I never knew you," "I know you not." The term *yada* is used to assert divine choice and appointment, as is evident from Gen. 18:19, as rendered by the Revisers, and substantially by Gesenius before them, "I have known him," *i. e.*, Abraham, "to the end that he may command his children and his household after him;" and γινώσκω, when used with the prefix προ, as in our passage, is employed to affirm the eternal choice and appointment of God, as is evident from 1 Pet. 1:20, as rendered in the Revision, where Christ as the chosen Lamb of God is thus spoken of, "Who verily was foreknown indeed before the foundation of the world," *i. e.*, as the Authorized Version has it, "foreordained before the foundation of the world." That προγινώσκω retains, as was to be expected, the pregnant meaning of γινώσκω and its Hebrew equivalent, is demonstrated by the passage just quoted, and by other instances in which it occurs, as, for example, in Rom. 11:2, "God did not cast off his people which he foreknew," *i. e.*, whom he fore-loved, fore-chose, and fore-recognized as his own.

The fuller senses of *yada*, and of γινώσκω with and without prefix, are a natural growth from their primary and literal sense of perceive or apprehend; and the usage with respect to corresponding words in other languages, English included, furnishes a broad analogy. As perception, or knowledge, real or imaginary, is the necessary condition of love, choice, appointment, and approval, these latter come by metonymy to be expressed in the terms belonging primarily to the former.

In the larger and fully authorized sense already indicated, the term "foreknew" is here to be taken; that alone being consistent with the apostle's argument and with the general character of his teaching. But which is the precise, or, rather, which is the more prominent, shade of this larger meaning, in which we should take the term, it is difficult with minute accuracy to determine. The best interpreters, though substantially in accord, vary considerably in detail. Erasmus takes the sense of the word as *foreloved;* Calvin, as *elected and adopted;* Alford, in *somewhat of the ordinary sense, with an implication of the larger meaning and in co-ordination with foreordination;* Tholuck, as *foredecreed,* in the earlier editions, but in the later, as *fore-recognized as his own;* Hodge, as *peculiarly loved and elected;* Brown, as *exercised peculiar and gracious complacency;* and Lange, though not defining it sharply, seems to regard the word as much the same as the Hebrew *yada* which he defines as "the one collective Hebrew term for knowing, loving, being present at, and begetting."

But with all their variety in form of statement, these interpretations, when analyzed and compared, are, in substance and logical effect, the same. Though apparently distinct as the billows, they are really one as the sea. They are not antagonistic, but complemental, and, to a certain extent, each implies every other. They all, in effect, repudiate the sense of mere naked prescience, and that of prescience of spiritual qualities, as the meaning of the term "foreknew," as here used; and, in effect, they all maintain that the word implies and expresses the eternal and distinguishing favor of God toward those whom, on this account, he determines eventually to save. These interpretations thus oppose the same errors, uphold the same truths, and cohere and inhere in one common centre of unity.

In view of all the facts, therefore, we need not hesitate to hold, with considerable confidence, that the term "foreknew," as used in this passage, declares, in a composite and ample sense, God's sovereign and eternal favor, love, choice, and recognition and acknowledgment as his own, in regard to those whom, for no possible reason in them, but for reasons immanent and hidden in himself, he, of his own good pleasure, predestined to salvation and eternal life. This much is demanded by the logic of the passage; and this much is sanctioned and accorded by the *usus loquendi* of Scripture and by the analogy of faith.

We may now proceed to consider the *second link* in the chain of grace, represented by the word προώρισεν, or "foreordained." The verb προορίζω occurs only six times in the New Testament, and it is translated uniformly in the Revision by the word "foreordain." The New Testament uses it to predicate a fixed pre-determination on the part of God as to the ordering of events and the final allotment of his people; and so, perhaps, the term "predestinated" employed here, and most frequently elsewhere, for it, by the Authorized Version, conveys the meaning more readily, on the whole, to the ordinary reader. Once, the word expresses God's foredetermining various things to come to pass in connection with the death of Christ. In the remaining five places in which it appears, it denotes the divine appointment of God's chosen people to a glorious destiny. In these instances, respectively, it declares them to have been foreappointed to divine sonship, to brotherhood, and likeness to Christ, to future glory, and to be to the praise of the glory of his grace. Here it teaches that all whom God "foreknew," that is, as we have seen, all whom he has eternally loved, chosen, and recognized and acknowledged as his own, are by him predestined to brotherly relations and likeness to Christ, his beloved Son, by all of which the glory of Christ, the Elder Brother, will be eternally advanced, and the blessedness of his younger brethren, the redeemed from among men, will be eternally promoted. This high destiny awaits all the true people of God. The means for its attainment are as truly foreordained as the persons are predestinated, and the end predetermined.

It is impossible that this sovereign and gracious decree of God should be frustrated or should in any way fail of final accomplishment, for he who is infinite in truth, in wisdom, and in power, has sworn, "My counsel shall stand, and I will do all my pleasure."[a]

We come now to the *third link* in the chain of grace, represented by ἐκάλεσεν, or "called." The word καλέω corresponds very closely, in ordinary parlance, to our English word "call," being used, as that is, to describe such acts as the giving or uttering of a name and the inviting or summoning of a person. Besides this, it is used in an efficient or causative sense, to which there is also some analogy in the use of the corresponding English word. In the Gospels it is sometimes, though rarely, used to denote the merely external call or invitation of the gospel. In the Epistles, however — and this is of the utmost doctrinal consequence — it is never so used. In them, when referring to the divine call of human souls, it is used invariably in the efficient or causative sense, and means inwardly, effectually, savingly called. It denotes the authority, energy, and efficacy, with which the Holy Spirit inwardly applies to human souls the outward call of the gospel, so as to result infallibly in their conversion to God, and in their translation out of the kingdom of darkness into the kingdom of God's dear Son. In the Epistles, the κλητοί, or "the

---

[a] Isa. 46:10

called," are widely distinguished from, and sharply contrasted with, those who have heard, but who have not accepted, the gospel invitation; as, for example, in 1 Cor. 1: 23, 24, where the apostle says, "We preach Christ crucified, unto Jews a stumblingblock, and unto Gentiles foolishness; but unto them that are called, both Jews and Greeks, Christ the power of God, and the wisdom of God." In the same strain, the true people of God are divinely addressed as distinctively the "called to be saints;" divinely declared to be "partakers of the heavenly calling;" and divinely exhorted to "walk worthily of the calling wherewith" they "were called."

There is a beautiful and suggestive connection between the terms, κλητοί, or the "called," and ἐκκλησία, or "the church," which deserves to be noticed, in passing. The κλητοί, as we have seen, are the savingly called, the genuinely converted; the ἐκκλησία, on the other hand, is the legitimate and constitutional assembly of the savingly called — called out authoritatively from their old relations to the world into organized unity, activity, and fellowship in the gospel.

The calling of this passage, therefore, is an effectual calling — a calling from death to life, from darkness into light, and from the power of Satan unto God.

The *fourth link* in the chain of grace, represented by ἐδικαίωσεν, or justified, now claims our attention. The writer of the Epistle to the

Romans, though a Jew by extraction, is a Roman by citizenship, and he is versed in Roman law and polity. He writes an Epistle expository of Christianity to Roman citizens, who, by their peculiar legal and political training, are specially capable of appreciating the meaning of words, the force of arguments, and the significance of analogies. In these circumstances, as might be expected from his marvellous tact and skill, he treats his subject forensically, especially as this method is really the most germane to his subject, and so he employs technical legal terms, well known to hisreaders, with which to set before them the central and fundamental truths of the gospel. The gospel truth which he most fully discusses is the cardinal doctrine of gratuitous justification by faith in the crucified Redeemer, and the term, therefore, which he employs to express it is one that is saturated with forensic meaning, inwrought with forensic associations, and practically incapable of being employed in any other than a forensic sense.

In the earlier part of the Epistle, the apostle proves that all men are under divine law, natural or revealed; that all men are sinners — transgressors of the law; and that all men, in their natural state, are therefore, actually, justly, and inevitably under its dread sentence of condemnation. He then proceeds to show that by means of the gospel God can accomplish what he could not accomplish by means of the law; that through the instrumentality of the gospel

GROUP OF PAULINE DOCTRINES. 221

he can do the very reverse of what he does, and must do, through the law without recourse to the gospel; that is to say, he can and does justify, through the gospel, many whom, under the law, he inevitably condemned.

To those who lived under the scientific, rigorous, and far-reaching Roman law, the term "justify" meant the act of a righteous judge toward accused persons proved innocent before him, in acquitting them and pronouncing them righteous; and the term continues to this day to be so used in systems of jurisprudence derived from the legal system of ancient Rome. This term the apostle deliberately employs to express what God actually does to condemned sinners who receive the gospel: God acknowledges and declares them to be, and treats them as, righteous. Just here lay the profoundest problem of redemption; and herein consists its mightiest achievement. How God could be just, and yet be the justifier of the unjust, none but himself could have devised. The gospel is his solution of the difficulty, and by it he is enabled both to be just and to justify every sinner who believes in Jesus.

We are forcibly taught, by the apostle, that this gospel justification, so far as the divine conferring of it on men is concerned, is absolutely a justification "by grace," and that from the very nature of the case, by grace alone could it possibly be conferred. But by the same decisive authority we learn that, so far as the divine procuring of it is concerned, gospel justification is not a mere arbitrary transaction, but that it is a justification "by blood," by the infinite and vicarious sacrifice and satisfaction made for us by the God-man to the law and justice of God. Thus "grace" reigns "through righteousness unto eternal life through Jesus Christ our Lord." Without this stupendous and unique provision, it would be as impossible for God to justify a sinner as to forsake his justice, to deny himself, or to cease to be.

The gospel is divinely declared to be "the power of God unto salvation to every one that believeth." But why? Because it reveals a divine righteousness receivable by faith; not the righteosness of the divine character; not a righteousness of divine requirements to be wrought out by every one for himself; not even a righteousness to be infused into the soul by the Spirit of God, but a vicarious righteousness planned by the Divine Father in his eternal counsels, executed in the fulness of time by the incarnate Son in his fulfilling the precept and in his exhausting the penalty of the divine law; revealed by the Holy Spirit in the gospel which he outbreathed, and freely imputed to the soul when effectually called by that Spirit into the exercise of living faith in Christ.

As far as human instrumentality in bringing this grace-given and blood-bought justification into personal possession is concerned, the Scriptures declare with full-voiced emphasis that it is received only by faith in Christ. From the various and vivid inspired descriptions of this justifying faith, abounding in Scripture, it is evidently not merely intellectual or speculative, but pre-eminently affectionate, moral, and spiritual in its character ; and so also it is at once a first-fruit of the regenerating Spirit, a spiritual ingrafting into the living Christ, and the prolific germ and the generous nourisher of all other spiritual qualities and virtues.

Justification being essentially, as we have seen, a judicial act of God respecting the personal, juridical standing of believers before his law ; being completed instantly at the first exercise of faith, and being of irrevocable and eternal validity, it is not to be confounded with forgiveness of sins, which, as distinguished from justification, is more properly a parental act of God, often repeated, often needing to be repeated, toward those whom, for Christ's sake, he once and forever absolves from guilt, justifies, and adopts as his children. Much less is justification to be confounded with sanctification ; for while the former is the divine reversal of a sinner's legal state, the latter is the divine renewal of his spiritual nature ; while the former is grounded on the imputation of righteousness, the latter is the means of the impartation of righteousness, or holiness ; and while the former is complete at the first moment of conversion, the latter is progressive throughout the entire subsequent life.

The *fifth link*—the final one in the chain of grace—represented by ἐδόξασεν, or " glorified," remains to be considered. At first sight the term "glorify," like the term "glory," seems somewhat vague in meaning. Like the first great verb in our chain of five, this last, in the apostle's use of it, is somewhat Hebraized, as a moment's consideration of it will suffice to show. The radical meaning of *kabod*, the principal Hebrew word for glory, is weight, heaviness; and the chief of its derived meanings are riches, honor, majesty, and splendor; so that it gives the conception of a person burdened and weighed down with opulence, splendor, honor, and dignity. Very prominent also in the Hebrew conception of glory is the element of brightness; and thus, in his golden diction, Ezekiel speaks of "the brightness of the Lord's glory," or rather "the brightness of the glory of Jehovah." How natural it was, therefore, that the chief inspired writer of the New Testament, when comforting sorrow-laden Christians on earth with the prospect of their heavenly destiny, should speak of it as "a far more exceeding and eternal weight of glory;" and that when exalting him who is at once the Jehovah of the Old Testament and the Jesus of the New, he should describe him as "the effulgence of" the Father's "glory."

In the term "glorify," or "make glorious," the dual conceptions of weight and brightness, substance and sheen, being constituents of the idea of glory, are present and predominant. The glorified are permeated with the bright essence and radiant with the bright effluence of infinite and eternal good. The glory of the redeemed is, in part, incipient during their earthly sojourn, though greatly shrouded and obscured; but its fulness and effulgence are reserved for the heavenly state. Even in this present life, however, the believer is glorified with the glory of divine sonship, though still in minority; with the glory of a regenerate and sanctified likeness to Christ, though yet incomplete and imperfect; with the glory of an inner life and abiding fellowship with God, though often beclouded and greatly circumscribed; and thus is fulfilled, partly at least, the saying of the Saviour in his prayer to the Father, "The glory which thou gavest me I have given unto them." At the close of earthly existence, despite the sinister shadows of death, the believer is glorified in being borne by angels from the tabernacle of clay to the heavenly mansion, from the grasp of the King of Terrors to the bosom of God, forever to abide in his love and in the light of his countenance. On his disentanglement from mortal life the believer's soul-likeness to Christ will instantly become complete, and the spiritual glory of his character will then be ineffable. At the last day the Christian will be glorified in the resurrection of his body from the vile dust of death to immortality and likeness to Christ's glorious body. Like some beauteous flower sprung from a seed that had shrivelled for ages in the cerements of a mummy, or like some insect that, having passed its unsightly rudimentary state, glances gaily in the sunbeams, all gleaming with crimson and gold, the Christian's body will be raised in unimagined glory, despite the dishonor in which it was sown. In soul and body, reunited and glorified, the redeemed will therefore be perfectly conformed to the image of Christ; and through all eternity, amid the society and splendor, the pursuits and enjoyments, of the heavenly state, they will exult in the presence, the glory, and the favor of Christ, and "shine forth like the sun in the kingdom of their Father." Doubtless the ultimate completion of the glorifying of believers in their heavenly state is the great strategic point directly and primarily indicated by this term of the apostle; but it also evidently implies and presupposes the quickening and sanctifying processes preparatory to, and, indeed, initiatory of, the final consummation.

Thus the great chain of grace, constituted, without one missing or faulty link, by divine foreknowledge, foreodination, calling, justification and glorification, unites the eternities of the past and future, unites the mighty truths of revelation, and makes doubly sure the assurance of the gospel's final success and of the believer's eternal salvation.

II.

DIVINE ESTIMATE OF THE PASTORAL OFFICE.*

There are now current a variety of influences tending to depreciate the pastoral office in the minds of possible ministerial recruits, in the minds of ministers themselves, in the minds of Christian people generally, and in the minds of all sorts of people of the world. Among these unfavorable influences are the supreme importance now commonly attached to wealth, the feverishly eager pursuit of it, characteristic of the time, the long and expensive period of preparatory study requisite for the best results of ministerial work, the general inadequacy of ministerial support, and the growing demand for highly sensational methods. In view of these things, and as far as may be to counteract them, it would be well if the churches of Christ, if Christian young men, and if the ministers of the gospel would consider attentively the divine estimate of the pastoral office.

1. The divine estimate of the pastoral office is indicated by the qualifications divinely prescribed for it. In various parts of the New Testament, particularly in the "pastoral Epistles" to Timothy and Titus, there are summaries and

* This discussion was published in the *Baptist Quarterly Review*, January, 1892, and it is here introduced by the author as a side-light on the pastoral office already considered in Section II. of our ninth chapter.

expositions of the rare combination of intellectual, moral, and spiritual qualities and attainments divinely required in those who enter the Christian ministry. These men must have certain natural and acquired abilities — capacity for study, aptness to teach, and talent for administration and leadership. They must be men of strong and consistent Christian character; their minds must be well stored with divine truth; their souls must be rich in ripe Christian experience; and their hearts must be filled with love and loyalty to the Saviour, with love and devotion to the church, and with earnest and compassionate desire for the salvation of sinners. They must not be novices, "lest being puffed up," they "fall into the condemnation of the devil," but they must be men tried, and proved worthy of confidence, of esteem, and of the high trust to be committed to them; men "full of faith and of the Holy Spirit;" "faithful men, who shall be able to teach others also." They must be men called of God into this service by a special work of grace in their own hearts, and by the voice of God summoning them to the office through his people. Well might any man exclaim, "Who is sufficient for these things?"

2. The divine estimate of the pastoral office may be perceived in the functions divinely assigned to it. The remarkable nomenclature employed by the Holy Spirit in speaking of the chief officer of a Scripturally-constituted church indicates unmistakably the variety and importance of the pastoral functions. The

Christian minister is commissioned as an "ambassador" of Christ; and, "as though God were entreating" men by him, he is required to proclaim the gospel message of reconciliation. He is sent of God, as a "preacher and teacher" of divine and saving truth. He is a "minister" or "servant" of Christ, and of the church for Christ's sake; but he is to serve the church, not as a menial or slave, but as an instructor, as a leader, as a presiding officer chosen by the church and appointed by Christ to act in these capacities for the good of the church and the glory of the Lord. He is a "presbyter" or "elder," charged with the work of counselling and guiding the church. He is made by the Holy Spirit a "bishop" or "overseer" of the church placed under his personal and official care. He is the "pastor" or "shepherd" of the flock, the church of Christ, appointed to this office by Christ, the Chief Shepherd. He is the "angel" of the church, that is, the "angel" or "messenger" of God to declare to the church the word of God, and to watch and guard the vital interests of the church and of the truth, in the Saviour's name.

The nurture, training, leading, and well-being of the church, and the conversion of sinners to Christ, are to be his constant care. Thus the functions of the pastoral office relate primarily and pre-eminently to supreme and eternal interests—the salvation of souls, the welfare of the church, and the glory of God.

3. The divine estimate of the pastoral office

is evinced by the regards for it, divinely enjoined. Esteem, love, deference, gratitude, intercession, are prominent among the Christian regards to be exercised toward those who, in the name of Christ, minister in holy things.

Upon this point, "What saith the Scripture?" "But we beseech you, brethren, to know them that labour among you, and are over you in the Lord, and admonish you; and to esteem them exceeding highly in love for their works' sake."[a] "Obey them that have the rule over you, and submit to them; for they watch in behalf of your souls, as they that shall give account; that they may do this with joy, and not with grief: for this were unprofitable for you."[b] "Touch not mine anointed ones and do my prophets no harm."[c] "Let him that is taught in the word communicate unto him that teacheth in all good things."[d] "Brethren, pray for us," "and on my behalf, that utterance may be given unto me in opening my mouth, to make known with boldness the mystery of the gospel."[e]

Two opposite temptations are liable to befall the Christian minister in relation to these divinely enjoined regards on the part of his people for his office. One of these is arrogantly to claim these regards as a personal right, to use them for his own gratification, instead of receiving them humbly as a trust from Christ to be used exclusively for the good of the church itself and for the honor of the Master.

[a] 1 Thess. 5:12. [b] Heb. 13:17. [c] Ps. 105:15. [d] Gal. 6:6. [e] Eph. 6:19.

The other is to refuse such regards and weakly throw them away, either from timidity, false humility, or excessive and selfish desire to please men.

But whatever the possible temptations in the case, it is strikingly significant that the divine word enjoins such regards for the pastoral office and its occupant.

4. The divine estimate of the pastoral office is manifest from the responsibilities divinely imposed upon it. The pastor, in virtue of his office, is brought into specially grave and responsible relations to the Judge of all; and the Scriptures abound with solemn admonitions and warnings to pastors. Very awe-inspiring is the warning of God to the divinely appointed spiritual watchman, whose business it is to hear the word at the lips of God and to warn men in his name: "When I say unto the wicked, O wicked man, thou shalt surely die, and thou dost not speak to warn the wicked from his way; that wicked man shall die in his iniquity, but his blood will I require at thine hand."[a] Equally searching and solemn is the apostolic admonition to the minister of the word: "I charge thee in the sight of God, who quickeneth all things, and of Christ Jesus, who before Pontius Pilate witnessed the good confession; that thou keep the commandment, without spot, without reproach, until the appearing of our Lord Jesus Christ."[b] The Lord will reckon with his ministers for the many impor-

[a] Ezek. 33:8.   [b] 1 Tim. 6:13, 14.

tant trusts he has committed to their charge; and he will hold them responsible for the manner and spirit in which they have discharged the various functions of their office. Better, far better, for a minister, that he never were born than to be unfaithful and unworthy, and to appear as such before the judgment-seat of Christ.

5. The divine estimate of the pastoral office is evident from the final rewards to be divinely bestowed upon it. Notwithstanding the difficulties, trials, and anxieties peculiar to the work of the gospel ministry, there are in this life itself many great and precious spiritual rewards for the faithful minister, in the character and privileges of the work, and in the special relationships of the pastor to Christ and to his true people. But the great rewards for the faithful discharge of this office are reserved for the future life. Near the close of the bright prophetic Book of Daniel we read: "They that be wise shall shine as the brightness of the firmament; and they that turn many to righteousness as the stars forever and ever."[a] In the address of Peter to the elders, Christian ministers who faithfully and lovingly fulfil the duties of their office are told, "When the chief Shepherd shall be manifested, ye shall receive the crown of glory that fadeth not away."[b] It was primarily to the "angel" or pastor of a church that the glorified Redeemer said, "Be thou faithful unto death, and I will give thee the crown of life."[c]

[a] Dan. 12:3. [b] 1 Pet. 5:4. [c] Rev. 2:10.

www.ingramcontent.com/pod-product-compliance
Lightning Source LLC
Chambersburg PA
CBHW020811230426
43666CB00007B/965